Egyptian Myth: A Very Short Introduction

VERY SHORT INTRODUCTIONS are for anyone wanting a stimulating and accessible way in to a new subject. They are written by experts, and have been published in more than 25 languages worldwide.

The series began in 1995, and now represents a wide variety of topics in history, philosophy, religion, science, and the humanities. Over the next few years it will grow to a library of around 200 volumes – a Very Short Introduction to everything from ancient Egypt and Indian philosophy to conceptual art and cosmology.

Very Short Introductions available now:

Available soon:

For more information visit our web site
www.oup.co.uk/vsi

Geraldine Pinch

EGYPTIAN MYTH

A Very Short Introduction

OXFORD
UNIVERSITY PRESS

OXFORD

UNIVERSITY PRESS

Great Clarendon Street, Oxford OX2 6DP

Oxford University Press is a department of the University of Oxford.
It furthers the University's objective of excellence in research, scholarship,
and education by publishing worldwide in

Oxford New York

Auckland Bangkok Buenos Aires Cape Town Chennai
Dar es Salaam Delhi Hong Kong Istanbul Karachi Kolkata
Kuala Lumpur Madrid Melbourne Mexico City Mumbai Nairobi
São Paulo Shanghai Taipei Tokyo Toronto

Oxford is a registered trade mark of Oxford University Press
in the UK and in certain other countries

Published in the United States
by Oxford University Press Inc., New York

British Library Cataloguing in Publication Data

Data available

Library of Congress Cataloging in Publication Data

Data available

ISBN 978-0-19-280346-7

5 7 9 10 8 6

Typeset by RefineCatch Ltd, Bungay, Suffolk
Printed in Great Britain by
Ashford Colour Press Ltd, Gosport, Hants

Contents

Acknowledgements

I would like to thank George Miller for commissioning this book; Dr Richard Parkinson for his cheerful help with queries about objects in the British Museum; and Professor Gay Robins and Dr Lisa Montagno Leahy for their advice and support. As always, I am grateful for the privilege of using Sackler Library, Oxford University, and to Professor John Baines for his inspirational teaching and encyclopaedic knowledge.

List of illustrations

The publisher apologizes for any errors or omissions in the above list. If contacted they will be pleased to rectify these at the earliest opportunity.

Introduction

In the late 4th millennium BC, the valley and delta of the River Nile were formed into the twin kingdoms of Upper and Lower Egypt. Over the next 3,000 years Egypt was ruled by 32 dynasties of kings (see the timeline at the end of this book). One title for an Egyptian king was Pharaoh (meaning 'Great House'), and so this great span of time is often known as the Pharaonic Period.

For much of the 3rd and 2nd millennia BC, Egypt was the wealthiest and most powerful nation in the Ancient Near East. The Egyptians were pioneers of monumental stone architecture. They produced magnificent sculpture and painted reliefs, and invented the hieroglyphic script, one of the world's earliest and most beautiful forms of writing. Even after Egypt lost its political independence in the late 1st millennium BC, its culture and religion survived to influence those of Greece and Rome.

Mythology was an integral part of Egyptian culture for much of its timespan. Characters and events from myth permeate Egyptian art, architecture, and literature. Myths underpinned many of the rituals performed by kings and priests. Educated Egyptians believed that a knowledge of myth was an essential weapon in the fight to survive the dangers of life and the afterlife.

There is disagreement among Egyptologists about when mythical narratives first developed in Egypt. This dispute is partly due to the difficulty of deciding what should be counted as a myth. Today, the term myth is often used in a negative way to refer to something that is exaggerated or untrue. In ancient cultures, myth did not have this negative connotation; myths could be regarded as stories that contained poetic rather than literal truths. Some scholars separate myths from other types of traditional tale by classifying them as stories featuring deities. This simple definition might work quite well for Egypt, but not for all cultures.

Myths are generally set in a remote time or place where humans and deities can interact. They are stories imbued with meaning and power. Myths could be used to explain or justify the way the world is. Even in modern times we acknowledge that a myth can take on a life of its own and become more influential than the original facts on which it was based. For the Egyptians, myths had the power to transcend individual experience and act as a bridge between the human and divine worlds.

Egyptian mythology never solidified into one standard version. It continued to change and develop over 3,000 years. The chief deities of regional temples generated their own myths. The basic events, which might be described as 'core myths' (see Box 1 in Chapter 1), were constantly retold and given many different actors and settings.

This book is arranged thematically, with each theme illustrated by a particular Ancient Egyptian artefact. These artefacts have been chosen to emphasize the diversity of the source material that Egyptologists work from. Hopefully, the objects will serve as access points to a culture that can seem very alien to the modern Western mindset. I shall not pretend that everything about Egyptian myth can be made simple. The complexity of this subject is what makes it endlessly fascinating to study.

Chapter 1

The myth of Egypt: imagined Egypts

The sources for Egyptian myth are not all dusty scrolls of papyrus. On the north bank of the River Thames in central London stands the monument known as Cleopatra's Needle (Figure 1). Though its elaborate base and surrounding sphinxes are Victorian, the 'needle' itself is a genuine obelisk from Ancient Egypt. The nickname, based on an Arab term for obelisks, reflects the popular idea that everything in Ancient Egypt was on a monumental and inhuman scale. At over 20 metres (68 feet) tall, Cleopatra's Needle belongs to the category of super-obelisks made for Egypt's greatest temples.[1] It fulfils the Western image of Egyptian architecture by being both grand and mysterious. The Egyptians had a gift for creating striking visual symbols to convey complex ideas. An obelisk is a sculptural representation of a mythological place and time.

The adventures of an obelisk

Cleopatra's Needle actually dates to the reign of King Thutmose III (*c.*1479–1425 BC), who lived around 1,400 years earlier than the Cleopatra everyone has heard of (Cleopatra VII). Thutmose's granite obelisk was one of a pair quarried in Aswan and floated 400 miles down the Nile to Heliopolis ('City of the Sun'). The pair were made to stand at the entrance to the great temple of the sun god, Ra. Solar mythology was crucial to Egyptian culture, so this was one of Egypt's most important temples. The priests of

1. Cleopatra's Needle (obelisk of Thutmose III) on the Thames embankment

Heliopolis were renowned in the ancient world for their knowledge and wisdom. Many of the myths discussed in this book may have originated in Heliopolis. The temple of Ra was later plundered to build Cairo. Its scant remains now lie under a modern suburb and the city's airport. Cleopatra's Needle is a sad reminder of how much of Egypt's heritage has been lost or displaced and how difficult it is to piece together the scattered remains.

By erecting these obelisks in Heliopolis, Thutmose III was carrying out one of the main functions of an Egyptian king. That function was to facilitate the daily cycle in which the sun god was thought to renew the universe. The tips of the obelisks were covered with an alloy of gold with silver, called electrum. The structures would have been sited so that the sun lit them up every morning. Together, the obelisks represented the place of renewal, the mountains of the horizon. Cleopatra's Needle is the western horizon, the place of sunset and death. The other obelisk of the pair is the eastern horizon, the place of dawn and rebirth. Like most Egyptian symbols, obelisks can represent more than one thing simultaneously. Individual obelisks also stood for the primeval mound, the place of the very first sunrise at the dawn of creation. They acted as markers of mythological time. The role of these obelisks as elements in a working model of the cosmos was obscured by their subsequent history.

In the 13th century BC, the famous ruler Ramesses II inscribed his name on the obelisks. They may have been moved to the Nile Delta at this time to stand in one of the temples he built or enlarged there. By the 1st century BC they were in Alexandria, the capital city of the Ptolemy dynasty, of which Cleopatra VII was the last representative. Alexandria was the intellectual hub of the Hellenistic world; a centre for science and philosophy. The presence of obelisks was a reminder of more elusive forms of knowledge which could not be tested by experiment or attained by rational argument. An inscription shows that the obelisks were re-erected under Cleopatra's nemesis, the Emperor Augustus, outside a temple dedicated to the cult of Julius Caesar. Eventually, one of Alexandria's frequent earthquakes toppled the western obelisk.

This obelisk was offered to Britain by a Turkish governor after the British had defeated Napoleon's army at the Battle of Alexandria in AD 1801. Cleopatra's Needle remained an uncollected present until AD 1877, when it was transported to Britain on the barge 'Cleopatra', with the loss of six lives on route. The successful erection of the obelisk on the Thames embankment inspired envy in America. So the other obelisk of the pair was transported to New York and erected in Central Park in AD 1881. Parted by an ocean, the function and meaning of Thutmose III's obelisks were lost. This was a fate shared by many Egyptian obelisks, but new meanings were assigned to them in new contexts. The first Egyptian obelisks had been moved to Europe in the reign of Augustus. They were used to adorn various monuments, including his tomb. This encouraged the idea that obelisks were principally monuments to the dead. In recent centuries, obelisks have frequently been used to mark tombs or commemorate war dead. Ancient Egypt has often been branded as a society obsessed with death, but Egyptian thought was not morbid. In their original setting, the obelisks celebrated the victory of life over death.

Secret wisdom

Obelisks are usually inscribed in the type of Egyptian writing known as hieroglyphs. By the end of the 4th century AD, there were very few people left who could understand the hieroglyphic script. Around this time an Egyptian named Horapollo wrote a treatise that popularized the idea that the hieroglyphic signs were an esoteric symbolic language which concealed great religious truths. As early as the 1st century AD, the Roman author Pliny the Elder had asserted that the Egyptians inscribed their most secret knowledge on obelisks. This knowledge was said to be nothing less than the nature of the universe and the meaning of life. The belief that the Egyptians possessed this secret is the primary myth about Ancient Egypt.

When Egypt became a Christian country in the 4th century AD, the 'pagan' culture of the Pharaonic past was rejected. In the Hebrew books of the Old Testament the polytheism of the Egyptians was contrasted unfavourably with the monotheism of the Jews. Early Christians continued to believe in the existence of pagan deities but downgraded them to the status of demons. The violence and sexuality of some of the myths told about Egyptian deities were used to support this view.

The Muslim Arabs who conquered Egypt in the 7th century AD were also hostile towards Ancient Egyptian religion. Arab scholars interested in alchemy did preserve some examples of the texts known as the Hermetica. These were produced in Egypt during the Graeco-Roman Period and are mainly written in Greek. They claimed to be the secret teachings of the great sage Hermes Trismegistus, a figure partially derived from Thoth, the Egyptian god of wisdom. The Hermetica mix Greek philosophy with Egyptian myth and give allegorical significance to magical and alchemic practices. They promise the secret of immortality to initiates who follow the teachings of Hermes.

Renaissance and Enlightenment

The great rediscovery of Classical learning in the Renaissance period made some information about Egyptian myth available. From the 6th century BC onwards, many famous Greek authors had written respectfully about Egyptian religion. The philosopher Plato credited Thoth with the invention of writing, mathematics, and astronomy. The myth of Atlantis, related by Plato in his dialogue *Timaeus* (*c*.348 BC), is attributed to a wise Egyptian priest who knew about a whole series of destructions going back to the early days of the universe. Later Classical tradition claimed that most of the great philosophers had studied at Heliopolis or other Egyptian religious centres.

The historian and philosopher Plutarch probably did visit Egypt during the 1st century AD. His book *Concerning Isis and Osiris* retells and interprets many myths about this important pair of deities. Sources like these gave rise to the habit of perceiving Egypt through Greek or Roman eyes. This has been particularly damaging for the study of Egyptian myth. Whatever the links between them, Greek and Egyptian mythology were very different in scope and function.

Renaissance scholars wrongly believed that the Hermetica were much older than the works of philosophers such as Pythagoras, Plato, and Aristotle. The Hermetica were thought to expound the most ancient and natural form of religion. One manifestation of a growing discontent with the corruption and brutality of the established Christian church was a desire to return to this lost golden age of religious thought. By the 17th century AD, scholarship had proved that the Hermetica were not in fact immeasurably ancient, but many still believed that primeval wisdom was concealed in the undeciphered hieroglyphic texts on Egyptian objects brought to the West. Secret societies such as the Rosicrucians and the Freemasons used Egyptian symbolism to lend a spurious antiquity to their beliefs and practices. Egyptian wisdom became associated with radical and anti-establishment groups, such as the leaders of the French Revolution, who replaced the hated Bastille prison with a 'Fountain of Regeneration' surmounted by an Egyptian goddess, and the founding fathers of America. Traces of the latter link still survive in the pyramid on the Great Seal shown on dollar notes and in the Washington Monument, the world's largest obelisk.

Egypt became more accessible to foreigners in the late 18th century AD, and large numbers of Egyptian antiquities were sent to

Europe. Pioneering scholars, such as those who accompanied Napoleon to Egypt, published illustrated accounts of ancient temples and tombs. Egyptian sculpture and painting became major influences on the decorative arts in Europe and America. The race to decipher Egyptian hieroglyphs was one of the great intellectual challenges of the early 19th century. Evangelical Christians hoped that Egyptian inscriptions would provide independent confirmation of events in the Bible. Proponents of the Enlightenment hoped that the same inscriptions would reveal an ancient philosophy to set against Christianity. Neither group was destined to be satisfied.

Decipherment and disillusion

Royal names inscribed on obelisks were among the first words written in hieroglyphs to be deciphered. Scholars of many nationalities played a role in the decipherment, but it was the brilliant French linguist Jean-François Champollion who made the greatest contribution. He laid the foundations for understanding the grammar of Ancient Egyptian as well as the scripts in which it was written. During the second half of the 19th century, huge numbers of Egyptian texts were translated into European languages for the first time.

It soon became clear that Ancient Egyptian religion had not been centred on a single holy book comparable with the Bible or the Koran. There were plenty of hymns and formulaic prayers but few texts that Europeans would classify as theology or philosophy. The vast majority of temple inscriptions proved to be about kings making standard offerings to gods. No collection of national myths and few long narratives of any kind were recovered. Such mythical narratives as did survive were mainly embedded in collections of funerary texts aimed at easing the transition into the afterlife or in magical spells for use in daily life. A relatively small number of mythical themes occurred over and over again in such sources (see Box 1).

Box 1

CORE MYTHS

Creator comes into being in the *nun* (primeval ocean)

First land (primeval mound) rises from the *nun*

Emergence of the sun god/birth of the solar child/first sunrise

Solar child is threatened by forces of chaos and saved by protective deities

Creation of living beings via the bodily fluids/thoughts/words/hands of the creator

Humanity springs from tears of angry Eye of Ra

Separation of earth god and sky goddess by air god

Creation of Egypt as part of the divine order

Continuing war between *isfet* (chaos) and *maat* (order)

The creator sun god loses his eye/daughter/defender, but she is persuaded to return

Rebellions by gods and people cause the sun god to destroy most of humanity and leave earth for heaven

Osiris, ruler of Egypt, is murdered by his brother Seth

The sisters of Osiris (Isis and Nephthys) search for his mutilated body

Isis revives the body of Osiris to conceive a son, Horus

The body of Osiris is mummified and protected from attacks by Seth

The divine mother gives birth to Horus in the marshes

The infant Horus is poisoned by chaos creatures and then healed

Horus and Seth fight for the right to rule

> **Seth is wounded in the testicles and Horus loses his eye/eyes**
>
> **The damaged eye of Horus is restored by another deity, usually Thoth**
>
> **Horus avenges his father; Seth is defeated or pacified**
>
> **Horus becomes king of the living; Osiris becomes judge of the dead and ruler of the underworld**
>
> **The sun god enters the underworld each night**
>
> **Deities and spirits defend the body of the sun god against the chaos monster Apophis**
>
> **The sun god unites with Osiris to raise the dead**
>
> **The sun god emerges at dawn to renew creation**
>
> **The creator grows weary and returns to the primeval ocean**
>
> **World returns to chaos**

Academics argue ferociously about what kind of stories myths are but usually agree that they are stories. In Egyptian art and literature individual mythical events, such as 'goddess gives birth to marvellous child', are often found on their own. Many different terms for these story elements or motifs are in use, such as mythemes, mythical statements, monomyths, and genotext. Much of this book will deal with mythemes rather than mythical narratives because mythemes are what anyone studying Egyptian culture will mainly encounter.

The difficulty of detaching Egyptian myth from its cultural context made it relatively unattractive to the 19th-century thinkers who were developing universal theories of myth. The exception was the school who saw myths as evolving to explain ancient rituals and customs, but they were mainly concerned with tracing the 'primitive' origins of myths. They had little interest in looking at how the myths functioned when Egyptian civilization was at its height.

Mystical and occult sects such as the Theosophical Society and the Hermetic Order of the Golden Dawn enthusiastically added Egyptian myth and magic to their hotchpotch of beliefs. This may be one reason why many Egyptologists trained in the late 19th and early 20th centuries AD treated Egyptian religion with disdain. Far from being pure and sublime, it was seen as intellectually inferior to monotheism and tainted with the 'cancer' of magic. The Egyptian priesthood, so admired by the Ancient Greeks, was condemned for performing pointless rituals and meddling in politics. Some Egyptian myths were regarded as embarrassingly crude because of their sexual content. The inscription on Cleopatra's Needle links the king who dedicated the obelisk with the god Ra-Atum who was said to have created the first life by masturbating and taking his semen into his mouth. Because of this myth, obelisks could be associated with the erect penis of the creator. No wonder Sigmund Freud collected Egyptian religious art!

Sir Alan Gardiner, author of the standard work on Egyptian grammar, remarked that some of the religious texts that he translated '..must appear to the modern mind as unmitigated rubbish'.[2] When he and his colleagues were accused of being 'unsympathetic and patronising towards the myths and religious practices of Pharaonic times', he replied that this was better than 'regarding priestly writings with respectful awe' simply because they came from Ancient Egypt.

In more recent times, Egyptologists have striven to treat Egyptian religion in a non-judgemental way. Cultural relativism, and the fact that religion no longer holds a central place in many people's lives, have encouraged this approach. In Continental Europe, mythology is still taken seriously as a key to the human mind. The tendency among Continental writers to concentrate on arguing about definitions and terminology can be off-putting to the general reader.

In the English-speaking world comparatively few Egyptologists now specialize in religion and myth. The current emphasis on studying the daily life of ordinary people is partly responsible for this. The art, architecture, and literature of 'high culture' are routinely dismissed as elitist. The methods by which obelisks were constructed and the people who erected them are more likely to be studied than the significance of obelisks in religion or myth.

Why study Egyptian myth?

The science of archaeology has replaced the aim of learning from the past with the aim of learning about it. All the objects and texts recovered by archaeology are now deemed to be of equal interest, though this is not the way that most intelligent people treat objects and texts of their own era. Myths were the products of Ancient Egypt's most original minds and deepest thinkers. This book will make no apology for believing that a reason to be interested in them. Egyptian myths articulate the core values of the first great nation-state and one of the longest-lasting civilizations in the history of our planet.

Myths helped people of all ranks to explore their mental world, resolve crises, and endure the contradictions of life. What the Egyptians thought and hoped and dreamed are surely at least as important as what they ate or wore. Myths are a valuable source of information on national preoccupations. To take just one example, the stories in which deities have to argue their cases before a divine tribunal demonstrate how important the concept of justice was in Egyptian society.

Myth was one of the elements of Egyptian culture that most impressed and influenced contemporary civilizations. Stories and symbols crossed national boundaries and were reinterpreted to suit their new settings. The mythology of Isis and Osiris gave rise to an international cult which was Christianity's main rival under the Roman Empire. Via Greece and Rome, Egyptian myth became part of Europe and America's cultural history, featuring in such diverse works as the poetry of Milton, an opera by Mozart, and the novels of Thomas Mann.

In the 21st century AD, more and more people are turning to the pagan past for spiritual inspiration. Among such seekers, mythical Egypt is a landscape of pyramids and obelisks, sphinxes and animal-headed deities, lost tombs and reanimated mummies. To find out how accurate this picture is, we must go back to the words of the Egyptians themselves.

Chapter 2
Divine words: language and myth

Our knowledge of Egyptian mythology has to be put together like a jigsaw puzzle. The pieces consist of hundreds of written and visual sources of many different dates. To make matters more complex, these sources are written in a variety of scripts and languages. Egyptologists recognize five main stages of the Egyptian language, and the Egyptians themselves devised four different scripts in which their language could be written (see Box 2). By far the best known of these is the hieroglyphic script which the Egyptians called *mdw ntrw* – 'divine words'. The word *twt* 'image' could be used for an individual hieroglyph or for a cult statue. Both were thought of as potentially alive.

Box 2

**LANGUAGES AND SCRIPTS USED IN
ANCIENT EGYPT**
4th millennium BC
Spoken and written language: Old Egyptian
Scripts in use: Proto-hieroglyphs; Hieroglyphic (from *c*.3200)

3rd millennium BC
Spoken and written language: Old Egyptian
Scripts in use: Hieroglyphic, Hieratic

2nd millennium BC
Spoken and written languages: Middle Egyptian; Late Egyptian (from *c.*1400 BC)
Scripts in use: Hieroglyphic, Cursive Hieroglyphic, Hieratic

1st millennium BC
Spoken languages: Late Egyptian, Demotic, Greek
Written languages: Neo-Middle Egyptian, Late Egyptian, Demotic, Greek
Egyptian scripts in use: Hieroglyphic, Hieratic, Demotic

1st millennium AD
Spoken languages: Demotic, Greek, Latin; Coptic (five dialects); Arabic (from 7th century AD)
Written languages: Neo-Middle Egyptian, Demotic, Coptic, Arabic
Egyptian scripts in use: Hieroglyphic, Demotic, Coptic

A magical stela

Egyptian belief in the power of the written word is exemplified by a beautifully preserved stela (a slab decorated with images and inscriptions) found during the digging of a well in AD 1828 (Figure 2a-b). It is the largest example of a type of stela known as a cippus, from a Greek word meaning 'shield'. The stela was given by the ruler of Egypt to the Austrian Chancellor, who installed it in Schloss Metternich. Thereafter the piece was known as the Metternich Stela. In AD 1950 it was acquired by the Metropolitan Museum of Art in New York.[1]

The centre panel features five deities who are prominent in Egyptian myth: (2a from left to right) Isis; Ra-Horakhty, the embodiment of the sun at its zenith; Horus the Child; a symbol representing the murdered god Osiris; and ibis-headed Thoth. Above them, and on the back of the stela, outlandish divine beings are arranged in registers. In the topmost register, the spirit of the sun god is adored by the eight baboons of the horizon and the reigning king. The main part and base are covered in inscriptions which continue on the back and sides (2b). These are in the pictorial hieroglyphic script.

When this stela was found, Champollion had only just announced his decipherment. It was hardly possible to tell images from text and this is not an entirely false impression. Text and images were integrated in complex ways. A translation of the text alone cannot do full justice to the meaning of the stela. The inscriptions on the stela were first edited and translated in the 1870s. They proved to contain a collection of 13 incantations, some of which incorporate mythical narratives about the poisoning and healing of deities.

One tells how Isis gave birth to Horus in the marshes. When she leaves him to find food he becomes very ill. The distraught Isis summons the marsh-people to help her. A local wise woman suggests that baby Horus has been bitten by a scorpion or a snake. Isis shrieks over and over again 'Horus has been bitten!'. Her cries stop the boat of Ra as it crosses the heavens. Thoth comes down from the Sun Boat to see what has happened. Isis complains that her innocent son has been poisoned. Thoth saves the future of the divine order by healing Horus with the 'breath of life'. He lists all the mysterious deities, such as 'the lion of darkness' and 'the noble scarab beetle', who will protect Horus and all other victims of poison. The spell ends with the promise that all suffering people and animals will be healed as Horus was once healed.

Carving lengthy hieroglyphic texts into hard stone was a very skilful and time-consuming process and was undertaken only for

2a. Drawing of the upper part of the Metternich Stela

2b. Back of the upper part of the Metternich Stela

important reasons. According to the inscriptions, a priest called Nesatum had the stela made in honour of the Mnevis bull, an incarnation of the sun god, and his king, Nectanebo II (c.360–343 BC). Nesatum claimed that the texts on the stela were ancient magical writings that he had found in the burial ground of the sacred Mnevis bulls at Heliopolis. Such claims usually have to be treated with suspicion, but the language of some of the texts shows that they were around 1,000 years old by the time they were copied onto the stela.

Instead of hoarding these healing spells in his private library, Nesatum put them on display in the outer area of a temple. His stela had both an esoteric and a practical function. On one level, the spells and images on the Metternich Stela played out the eternal war between order and chaos that was a central part of Egyptian myth. On another level, they provided remedies for everyday hazards such as snake and scorpion bites. Many of the deities on the stela are shown trampling, spearing, or strangling snakes, crocodiles, and other dangerous creatures. Any Egyptian would have recognized that these bizarre figures were the traditional defenders of the sun god who were evoked to drive away evil and pain.

Words of power

The majority of Egyptians would not have been able to read the hieroglyphic inscriptions on the Metternich Stela, any more than the majority of medieval Christians could read the Latin inscriptions in their churches. Even if the stela inscriptions were read aloud to visitors by temple scribes, they might still have been difficult to understand because of their archaic language. The stories that form part of some of the spells are closer to the spoken language of ordinary people. They may have been recited or even acted out during temple festivals.

The power thought to be inherent in the words and images could be accessed by touching them. On some cippi the central figures have been almost rubbed away by the touch of anxious hands. Another method was to pour water over the cippus. The patient then drank or bathed in this water to receive a transfer of life-giving energy. We think of the written word as something that is primarily read in silence and solitude. The Metternich Stela is a reminder that things were very different in Ancient Egypt.

Myths are often defined as 'sacred stories', so it might be assumed that they were always written in the 'sacred' hieroglyphic script, but this is very far from the case. The power thought to reside in this script made the Egyptians cautious about how they used it. Myths tend to focus on trouble and conflict in the divine realm. To put an evil act, such as the murder of Osiris by his brother Seth, into hieroglyphs could make it a permanent part of reality. Direct descriptions or representations of such acts were usually avoided.

The story preserved on the Metternich Stela does relate how Horus was poisoned, but it comes complete with a happy ending. Even then, the divine suffering described in the hieroglyphic text has to be counterbalanced by dozens of positive images of deities overcoming chaos-beasts. King Nectanebo appears on the stela as an intermediary between the gods and the people who sought healing. One of the main purposes of the hieroglyphic script was to allow kings to communicate with gods and ancestors on behalf of humanity. To understand this we will have to look back at the history of writing in Egypt.

Writing and royalty

Hieroglyphs were both a practical means of communication (see Box 3) and a system for classifying the world. Individual hieroglyphs are pictures of the deities, people, animals, plants, and objects which made up that world. The script was probably invented at the court of the southern kings who ruled most of Egypt by the late 4th millennium BC. The earliest hieroglyphs are on labels recording tax payments, royal possessions, and gifts made by the king to temples of the gods. During the early 3rd millennium BC, longer hieroglyphic texts were inscribed on stone buildings, statues, and stelae. It became standard to use the hieroglyphic script for inscriptions in temples and tombs and for royal pronouncements addressed to the gods or posterity. Boys were trained to read and write hieroglyphs in schools attached to palaces, royal burial grounds, and state-run temples. Nearly all of this educated elite went on to work for the government, often on projects such as pyramid building which emphasized the unique status of the king.

By the Old Kingdom (*c*.2686–2181 BC), the Egyptians had invented a writing paper made from papyrus and developed a simplified script, known as hieratic, which was used for letters and administrative documents. The creation of a hieroglyphic text on stone was a group project, but a hieratic text on papyrus was usually the work of a single scribe. Once hieratic started to be written in lines instead of columns, it became the main script for medical, magical, and literary texts (for an example, see Figure 7 in Chapter 7). Early versions of some of the spells on the Metternich Stela are written in hieratic.

No long narratives about deities survive from the Old Kingdom, but traditions about them may have been passed down orally. A huge number of gods and goddesses feature in a collection of spells from royal pyramids of the 24th to the 22nd centuries BC. These 'Pyramid Texts' often allude to mythical events, such as the creator Atum spitting or sneezing out the first pair of deities, Shu and Tefnut. The collection consists of five major categories of spell, including anti-snake spells of the type found on the Metternich Stela. The Pyramid Texts were not put together to explain the divine world or humanity's relationship with it. Their primary purpose was the transfiguration of the dead king or queen in whose pyramid they were inscribed. One method of achieving this was to ritually identify the deceased royal with characters and events in the divine realm.

Box 3

HOW HIEROGLYPHS WORK

The hieroglyphic script is not a childlike picture language but a sophisticated and flexible system deploying several different categories of sign. A single hieroglyph (sign) is sometimes used as an ideogram to represent a whole word. Thus the word for bull (*ka*) can be written with a picture of a bull with a stroke after it ⛫ ⎥. Hieroglyphs can also be phonetic, representing between one and four sounds. An owl 𓅓 writes 'm' and a piece of crocodile skin ⬭ writes 'km'. The 25 signs which each represent a single consonant or semi–vowel are often called the 'hieroglyphic alphabet', but this alphabet was never used on its own.

Words spelled out with phonetic signs usually end with a non-phonetic sign which clarifies the meaning of a word or the category it belongs in. For example, the eye hieroglyph ⬯ is placed at the end of words for sight or blindness. Such signs are known as determinatives or classifiers. When the eye hieroglyph is found at the beginning of a word, it may be writing the sound *ir* from *irt*, the Egyptian word for an eye. The *t* on the end makes *irt* a female noun, so when the eye of the creator is personified it becomes a goddess rather than a god. Word-play could generate myths. As the word for people sounded like the word for tears, humanity was said to be born from the tears of the eye goddess.

The way in which the language is written can provide evidence for the mythological roles of deities. The monster who represents the god Seth 𓄡 is used as a determinative for the word that means confusion. The names of all goddesses

can be determined with a cobra. The solar disc hieroglyph ⊙ |
spells *ra*, the Egyptian word for the sun and the name of the
sun god, but as a determinative it is used with words to do
with time. The names of gods are usually followed by a seated
figure of a deity 𓀭 . The fact that this is rarely included in
writings of Ra shows how closely this god was associated with
the light of the sun. Ra was so important in the divine hierarchy that his name may be shown first in a phrase or title
even when grammatically it should come at the end. Subtle-
ties of this kind are lost when a hieroglyphic text is translated
into English.

In spite of the god-like status claimed by kings, the Old Kingdom
ended with the decline and collapse of central authority. Some
Egyptologists have traced the great mythical theme of the war
between order and chaos to the shock of this collapse.

A golden age

A century of disunity was ended by a king from the Upper Egyptian
city of Thebes. The ensuing Middle Kingdom (*c.*2055–1650 BC)
is generally regarded as the golden age of Egyptian literature. A
wide range of prose and poetry written in Middle Egyptian survives.
Middle Egyptian continued in use as a literary language for around
2,000 years. This is why a priest like Nesatum could read and
understand ancient texts; educated Egyptians were not cut off from
their past by a language barrier.

During the Middle Kingdom, elite burials could include coffins
inscribed with elaborate spells to help the deceased in the afterlife
(see, for example, Figure 5 in Chapter 5). These spells, collectively
known as the Coffin Texts, contain even more allusions to mythical
events than the Pyramid Texts. Some of the spells consist of

speeches by deities relating things they have done or suffered. In many cultures the oldest tellings of myths are first-person narratives, a form that arises naturally from oral tradition. The Coffin Texts also include dialogues between deities, which give more than one viewpoint on mythical events.

Dialogues also feature in the genre known as Instruction or Wisdom Texts in which an authority figure (a god, king, or father) instructs a pupil on how to live according to the rules of *maat* (order, truth, justice). Some of these texts are realistic enough to acknowledge that the younger generation, who do not share the experiences on which their elders' beliefs are based, will probably reject the advice they are given. These are generally classed as ethical rather than religious texts, but they are full of references to myths.

A small number of stories survive from the Middle Kingdom, including part of a tale about Seth's attempted seduction of his nephew Horus. These early stories did not enjoy the high status of Instruction Texts, but they are far from being simple or clumsily told. 'The Shipwrecked Sailor' (*c.*1900 BC) is a tale of disaster overcome, told to cheer up an official in trouble with his king. The plotline, in which a sailor stranded on a remote island is saved by a mysterious snake, reworks a myth about the end of the world found in the Coffin Texts. In a surprising twist, the official refuses to cheer up, rejecting a view of the world where justice rules and the good are helped by the gods. By the Middle Kingdom, Egyptian authors were displaying a distanced attitude to myth and using it creatively to express ideas about a person's role in society.

A story cycle preserved in Papyrus Westcar (*c.*1700 BC) may be closer to popular oral tradition, but it has a complex structure. The story is set at the court of King Khufu (Cheops), the builder of the Great Pyramid. His sons entertain the king by recounting tales of great magicians who served Khufu's royal ancestors. One of the princes caps this by telling of a peasant called Djedi whose magic is more powerful than any magician of the past. When the feisty 110-year-old magician visits court he has a battle of wills with Khufu over the proper uses of magic. Djedi prophesies that three marvellous children are about to be born. The story then shifts to the house of a priest, whose wife Ruddjedet is experiencing a difficult labour. The sun god Ra, who seems to be the children's true father, sends deities disguised as a group of dancing girls and their porter to help Ruddjedet. After the triplets are born the deities leave three crowns hidden in the house.

The original audience would have known that Ruddjedet's children were destined to be the kings who replaced Khufu's dynasty. Egypt's long history made it possible to set fantastic stories far in the past. It was also permissible to portray kings of the past in an unflattering way for didactic purposes. Around the time of Papyrus Westcar, there was another decline in royal authority. During this Second Intermediate Period (*c.*1650–1550 BC), foreign rulers known as the Hyksos took control of the Delta. The Hyksos were eventually driven out by a Theban dynasty, and Egypt was reunited.

Innovations in the New Kingdom

During the New Kingdom (*c.*1550–1069 BC), Egypt acquired an empire in Nubia and the Near East and was at the height of its cultural vigour. Rulers like Thutmose III, the dedicator of Cleopatra's Needle, spent the wealth flowing in from the empire on a massive temple-building programme. The New Kingdom royal tombs in the Valley of the Kings were modest in scale but beautifully decorated by a community of artists and scribes who lived at Deir el-Medina. Texts now known as Underworld Books were copied from scrolls kept in temple libraries on to the walls of royal tombs. The central theme of these books was the journey of Ra. At night the sun god was believed to enter a dangerous realm where the enemies of the divine order tried to prevent him from reaching the eastern horizon to renew the world at dawn. In most

Underworld Books a series of captioned pictures replaced a written narrative.

Pictures were also of great importance in the New Kingdom collection of funerary texts now called the Egyptian Book of the Dead. Many owners of Books of the Dead would have been unable to read the hieroglyphic texts, but they could understand the complex vignettes that summarized the content of the spells. By the end of the New Kingdom, some elite burials included 'Mythological Papyri'. These illustrated mythical events, such as the separation of earth and sky, which had rarely been shown before.

Around the 14th century BC, a new form of the written language was introduced for informal texts. Late Egyptian was closer to the way that people actually spoke and it reflected a more ethnically diverse society. Only a small number of Late Egyptian stories are known, but they are of remarkable interest. Some survive in copies from Deir el-Medina, showing that literature was enjoyed by the newly prosperous 'middle class'. A lively narrative about the rivalry between Horus and Seth will be examined in detail in Chapter 7. The Late Egyptian stories known as 'The Doomed Prince' and 'The Tale of the Two Brothers' have been described as the world's oldest fairy tales because they include motifs, such as a princess imprisoned in a tower or a magician hiding his heart in a tree, which are found in the folklore of later cultures. 'The Tale of the Two Brothers' belongs to a peculiarly Egyptian genre in which mythical events seem to be re-enacted by human or semi-human characters.

Turbulent times

The New Kingdom ended with power divided between kings of Libyan descent in the north and the Theban priesthood in the south. During the 1st millennium BC, Egypt endured civil wars and a series of foreign invasions (see the timeline at the end of the book). A period of rule by a Nubian dynasty was ended by a brutal Assyrian invasion. In the 7th century BC, the Assyrians were driven out by an

Egyptian dynasty from Sais. Around this time a new script known as Demotic was introduced for everyday purposes. The same Greek term (meaning 'common') is used for a stage of the Egyptian language. A wide range of Demotic literature developed, some of it showing Greek influence. Tantalizing fragments of many story cycles and epics survive.

In the 5th century BC, the Persians conquered Egypt, but Egyptian leaders fought back with the aid of Greek mercenaries. For a time Egyptian-born kings ruled again. The Metternich Stela dates to the very last of these kings, Nectanebo II. In times of trouble, the Egyptians tended to look back to their glorious past. Nesatum emphasized that his spell collection was very old to give it authority and power. The spells created a version of the past in which *maat* always triumphed. His stela would have conveyed the message that the educated elite were still in charge and able to offer temple visitors access to ancient wisdom.

Only a few years after the Metternich Stela was set up, the Persians invaded again. Nectanebo fled, and many temples were plundered. Egypt next became part of the short-lived empire of Alexander the Great (356–323 BC). Ptolemy Lagus, one of Alexander's Macedonian generals, founded the dynasty that was to rule Egypt from Alexandria for nearly 300 years. During the Ptolemaic Period, Greek became the language of the administration, but Egyptian culture continued to flourish in temples. The Ptolemies contributed to a huge temple-rebuilding programme. This was continued for a century or so after Egypt became part of the Roman Empire in 30 BC.

Last days

The period from around 400 BC to AD 100 was an important one for the sources of Egyptian myth. Some myths and legends were expanded into elaborate literary narratives, regional myths were recorded in illustrated scrolls, and a few mythical narratives or dramas were inscribed in hieroglyphs on temple walls. A fear that Egypt's culture was under threat from outsiders may have stimulated this impulse to collate and preserve the country's myths. Many foreigners were genuinely interested in Egyptian religion, but they could not read the texts inscribed on temple walls or the books kept in temple libraries. Authors like Plutarch had to rely on stories that he, or earlier Classical writers, had been told by Greek-speaking Egyptians.

A script using the letters of the Greek alphabet with the addition of a few Demotic signs evolved around the 1st century AD. Some Hermetic and magical texts were written in this Coptic script, but most of the surviving literature in Coptic is Christian. By the 4th century AD, Christianity was the dominant religion in Egypt. Spells like those on the Metternich Stela were still used, but Isis and baby Horus were replaced as the main characters by Mary and baby Jesus. Modern Western ideas about divinity have been shaped by monotheistic religions such as Christianity. In the next chapter we will look at what the Egyptians thought about their deities.

Chapter 3
The gods themselves: deities and myth

The deities of Ancient Egypt are better known from their appearances in art than in myths. One of the masterpieces displayed in the Luxor Museum is a calcite pair statue showing King Amenhotep III (c.1391–1353 BC) embraced by the crocodile god 'Sobek-Ra, Lord of Sumenu' (Figure 3).[1] The seven-ton statue was found in a sealed pit in Dahamsha (ancient Sumenu) in AD 1967. The pit may once have been a temple pool where sacred crocodiles were bred. While most visitors to the museum can appreciate the technical brillance of this statue, its subject matter is of a kind that puts many people off Egyptian art. The dominance of royalty is now seen as sycophantic and politically primitive. Modern viewers often find images of animal-headed deities ridiculous or even repugnant, just as many ancient Greeks and Romans did. Classical art has its gods and monsters, but in Egypt the monsters seem to be the gods.

These attitudes are partly based on a misunderstanding of Egyptian art. Like much modern abstract art, Egyptian art is concerned with capturing the essence of a thing and with giving a tangible form to complex ideas. Amenhotep III was portrayed not as he happened to be but as the godlike youth and ideal ruler that Egypt needed. This meant that a century later Ramesses II was able to transform the piece into a statue of himself simply by carving his own name in place of Amenhotep's.

3. Pair statue of Sobek-Ra and Amonhotep III in the Luxor Museum

Sobek-Ra was an entity who combined the essence of two deities: the crocodile god and the sun god. This dual god is depicted as part animal to convey his strange and awesome divine powers. In particular, he has the strength, cunning, and longevity of the crocodile and power over the life-giving waters of the Nile. The solar disc in the headdress conveys that Ra, god of life-giving light, is manifesting himself in his form of Sobek. He is depicted as part human to allow him to interact with the king and offer him the *ankh*, the symbol of life. The statue group is intended to show, and by showing to bring about, the desired loving relationship between the king, representing humanity, and Sobek-Ra, representing the gods.

How was the nature of these gods expressed in myth and how different were they from Judaeo-Christian or Islamic ideas of the divine? A series of questions may help to clarify these issues.

Where did the gods live?

Did Egyptian deities dwell in some unreachable divine realm beyond space and time, or did they inhabit the human world? There is evidence for a variety of answers to this question. A few religious texts speak of the creator god Amun as an invisible, unknowable force existing beyond the limits of the cosmos. Others emphasize that something of the essence of the creator was present in the elements that made up the cosmos and in all the beings whom he had made.

One answer to where did the gods live might be 'in the past'. In a letter to his dead wife, a scribe called Butehamun refers to Ra and his ennead, or council, as being gone like the kings of old. Most of the surviving mythical narratives are set in a remote era when a dynasty of gods ruled Egypt. This golden age was terminated by the first acts of rebellion and murder (see Box 1).

Gradually, the gods withdrew to divine realms beyond and below the earth. There they lived in their mysterious true forms, as huge, radiant beings with an overpoweringly sweet scent. Most humans could only enter the divine realms after death, but deities continued to interact with the human world in a variety of ways.

Deities could manifest themselves in natural phenomena such as storms, floods, and plagues. Their spirits could be 'resident' in special or unusual people, such as kings and dwarfs, and in sacred animals, trees, and objects. One of the main functions of Egyptian art was to provide temporary bodies for deities in the form of statues, drawings, or hieroglyphs. Much of the ritual that went on in Egyptian temples was aimed at encouraging the gods to inhabit these bodies so that their presence could benefit humanity. Thus, a deity like Sobek could be thought of as living simultaneously in the primeval ocean before creation, in a palace in the mountains of the horizon, in wild areas of Egypt's lakes and marshes, and in the statues and sacred crocodiles kept in his temples.

How many deities did the Ancient Egyptians have?

Experts on Egyptian religion have given answers to this question that range from 'one' to 'thousands'. Egyptian religion is generally considered to have been a sophisticated form of polytheism. Right from the beginning it had many deities of both genders. People were free to worship or placate those manifestations of the divine that seemed most relevant to their lives. For example, if you made your living on the Nile, the crocodile god might be the focus for your devotions.

In the course of Egyptian history, about 80 deities had shrines or temples built for them in more than one place. Some deities, such as the sky goddess Nut, were rarely the subject of a cult but were very prominent in myth. Putting the evidence of cult and myth together, about 30 gods and goddesses could be described as major national deities (see Box 4).

The Egyptian word *ntr* (god or power) was used for these major deities and for numerous lesser beings, such as star gods, personified concepts, deified kings, the denizens of the underworld, and the bizarre protective beings shown on objects like the Metternich Stela. If all these entities are included in the pantheon, there are hundreds of named deities. If each manifestation of a deity worshipped at a particular place, such as 'Sobek-Ra, Lord of Sumenu', was counted separately, the list would run into thousands. Egyptian myth has a large potential cast of characters.

Some Egyptologists have argued that from primitive beginnings Egyptian religion developed into a type of monotheism. Egyptian ethical texts simply refer to god in the singular as the force that rules the universe. Creation myths show that the Egyptians believed in a primeval being who had created an infinite number of deities, people, and animals. From the New Kingdom onwards, some texts treat the whole Egyptian pantheon as merely souls or forms of this primeval creator. The heretic King Akhenaten (*c*.1352–1336 BC) tried unsuccessfully to abolish all deities except Aten, a solar creator god. His successors accepted that within the great cycle of creation, the divine was always manifest in numerous gods and goddesses.

Each of these deities could split into a pair or group, or merge with another deity. Some Egyptian texts praised Sobek-Ra as the one creator god. Others, such as the hymns dismissed as 'unmitigated rubbish' by Gardiner, listed the numerous forms of Sobek existing in various parts of Egypt. Sobek and Ra could merge into a solar-crocodile-creator, as in our statue, but both Ra and Sobek continued to function separately. The fluid way that deities were treated in Egyptian thought probably worked against the development of narrative myths.

Box 4

MAJOR DEITIES IN MYTH AND CULT

Amun/Amun-Ra – Creator deity, worshipped at Thebes as King of the Gods

Anubis – Jackal god, inventor of mummification and guardian of cemeteries

Atum/Atum-Ra – Creator deity of Heliopolis and evening form of the sun god

Bastet – Feline goddess, defender of Ra and bestower of fertility

Geb – Earth god, consort of Nut and head of the divine tribunal

Hathor – Cow goddess of birth, death, and cosmic renewal

Horus – Sky falcon, opponent of Seth and archetypal ruler of Egypt

Isis – Widow of Osiris, mother of Horus and Mistress of Magic

Khepri – Scarab god of dawn and renewal

Khnum – Ram god, creator deity and controller of the Nile flood

Khonsu – Creator moon god and controller of Fate

Maat – Daughter of Ra and goddess of truth and justice

Min/Amun-Min – God of male sexuality and agricultural fertility

Mut – Avenging goddess worshipped at Thebes as consort of Amun-Ra and mother of Khonsu

Neith – Creator goddess and defender of the sun god

Nekhbet – Protective vulture goddess of the south

Nephthys – Sister of Isis and unwilling wife of Seth

Nun – God of the primeval ocean

Nut – Sky goddess and mother of Osiris, Isis, Seth, and Nephthys

Ogdoad of Hermopolis – Eight primeval deities, including Amun and Nun

Osiris – Ruler of the underworld and god of crop fertility

Ptah – Creator god of Memphis and patron of artists and craftsmen

Ra – Creator sun god and Ruler of the Universe

Sekhmet – Ferocious solar lion goddess

Seth – Enemy of Osiris, rival of Horus, and strongest of the gods

Shu – God of air and sunlight who separated the earth and the sky

Sobek – Primeval crocodile god and Lord of the Nile

Sokar – Memphite god of death and regeneration

Tefnut – Sister of Shu and mother of Geb and Nut

Thoth – Lunar god of wisdom, language, and writing, with ibis and baboon forms

Wadjyt – Protective cobra goddess of the north

Were goddesses less powerful than gods?

To worship both male and female deities was the normal pattern for ancient religions. Even Judaism seems to have had a goddess who was the consort of Yahweh (a Hebrew word for God) before she was edited out of the textual record. The division into two main genders reflected the world as experienced. In that real world, Egyptian women did not share all the privileges of men. In myth, goddesses rarely seem inferior in power to gods. Most Egyptian creation myths made the creator primarily male, but some featured a primarily female creator, such as Neith, 'the mother and father of all things'. In theory, all deities were supposed to be obedient to the kingly sun god Ra, but by the New Kingdom Ra had a female counterpart known as Raiyet.

In some myths, Ra seems dependent on the power of his ferocious daughter, the eye goddess. She was created when Ra-Atum sent his eye to search for his lost children, Shu and Tefnut, in the darkness of the primeval ocean. When she returned, the eye goddess wept to discover that Ra had grown another eye. It was from these tears that humanity originated.

Goddesses were quite often defined in terms of their relationship with a male deity. When they were worshipped as part of a pair, the female name was usually placed second, as it would have been with a human couple. However, if the goddess was playing a maternal role, the child deity was given the inferior position. The maternal role was more important for goddesses than the paternal role was for most gods. Romantic love is almost entirely absent from Egyptian myth, but maternal love was consistently portrayed as one of the most powerful forces in the universe.

The restrictions on religious art can make goddesses look misleadingly passive. In art, Isis appears as a co-wife, mourning Osiris or standing deferentially behind his throne, and as a mother, sweetly nursing her baby son. In myth, she is a dominant figure who fights to avenge her husband and plots to place her son on the throne of Egypt. In art, goddesses seem to have a wider range of physical forms than most gods. Their shape-changing abilities were also celebrated in myth. In one mythical episode, Isis changes from old crone, to young girl, to bird of prey (see Box 9 in Chapter 7).

The dual nature of the eye goddess, who dealt out both life and death, could be expressed in sudden changes of form. When Ra sent his eye to destroy humanity for the crime of rebellion, she was transformed into the raging lioness, Sekhmet. She devoured all the evil humans and had to be tricked by Ra into sparing the rest. Her full lion form was vividly described in myth but very rarely shown in art. In general, goddesses were feared more than gods; there were no meek divine housewives in the Egyptian pantheon.

Was the Egyptian pantheon arranged into families?

Most Egyptians were less aware than we are of being unique individuals. They preferred to characterize themselves as being part of a family or hierarchical group, and seniority was respected. Egyptian deities often function in groups. In the presence of a senior god such as Ra, who is credited with kinglike authority, the others deities usually act like subservient courtiers.

Kinship terms were used rather loosely in Egypt, so when a god or goddess was called a son or daughter of Ra, this may mean only descendant or younger relative. The most famous group of Egyptian deities, the Ennead of Heliopolis, combined major elements of religious thought by fitting Osiris and Horus into the family tree of Ra-Atum. The four, or sometimes five, generations in this family tree span cosmic history from the creation of the world to the establishment of kingship (see Box 5). Deities could also be

---

Box 5

THE ENNEAD OF HELIOPOLIS

Atum/Ra-Atum

Shu – Tefnut

Geb – Nut

Osiris Isis Seth Nephthys

Horus

Some versions of this Ennead substitute Horus the Elder, a brother of Osiris and Seth, for Horus son of Isis.

---

arranged in what appear to be nuclear families, most commonly a triad of father, mother, and son. It would be a mistake to take such families too literally. There is rarely much consistency in these relationships. With a few exceptions, Egyptian deities are not fixed characters with fixed life histories. The most famous divine couple is Osiris and Isis, but Osiris was sometimes the husband of both his sisters, and Isis could be the sexual partner of her son Horus.

Most deities played particular roles, such as father, consort, or son, in relation to a wide range of other deities. In myth, Sobek was usually the son of the creator goddess Neith. At one of his cult centres he was paired with the snake goddess Renenutet, while Horus the Child took the role of their son. At another, Sobek was paired with the goddess Hathor, with the moon god Khonsu as the junior member of the triad. This pairing may have come about through association with the Nile, as Hathor could be linked with the Nile flood and with the north wind needed for sailing upriver. When Sobek was merged with Ra, his relationship with Hathor becomes more complex. In myth, Hathor could have a triple aspect as the mother, consort, and daughter of Ra; she was the eternal female complement of the sun god.

What are they deities of?

It has been traditional for scholars who study polytheistic systems to classify deities as being the gods or goddesses of some natural phenomenon or particular area of responsibility. Zeus, for example, is labelled as a sky god, and Aphrodite as the goddess of love. Such labels are useful for us (see Box 4) but may not correspond with the way that these deities were seen by their original worshippers. For the Egyptians, deities were first and foremost possessors of power. They could all be prayed to about anything, but there was some degree of specialization. The nature of a deity could be expressed by their names and epithets, by their appearance, and by the roles they played in myth.

Epithets of place were the most common, such as Sobek, Lord of Sumenu. Some gods and goddesses were simply the presiding spirits of a particular town, area, or local feature. Minor deities, such as Sia, god of creative thought, were merely personifications of concepts that would remain abstract in other cultures. Maat, the goddess who personified the divine order, began this way but developed into a more rounded figure in myth as the favourite daughter of the sun god. Other deities were linked to elements of the natural world but not in a simplistic way. The sun was only the visible manifestation of the glory of Ra, who defeated death and gave light and energy to all beings. Myth gave Ra another dimension as a fallible ruler saddened by revolts among humans and conspiracies among the gods. Some deities were associated with particular skills or areas of human experience, such as Thoth with writing, Isis with mourning and healing, and Hathor with love. These associations could generate myths.

Major deities usually had several spheres of interest, some of which overlapped with those of other deities. Few of Sobek's characteristics were exclusive to him, but together they formed a unique divine profile: he shared his crocodile form with other gods such as Seth and Khenty-khet; like Seth, he could be regarded as the strongest of the gods; like Min, he was the most virile of the gods, able to satisfy any number of goddesses; like Hapy, the spirit of the inundation (annual Nile flood), he was praised for 'greening' the desert; he was a local god to people in the Fayum area who lived around a lake full of crocodiles; he was the protector of those who worked on or near water, such as fishermen, bird-catchers, and washermen; he was the brutal instrument of fate who snatched people to sudden deaths; he was one of the creatures who embodied the primeval ocean; wearing his 'solar disc' hat, he was the deity who created and sustained the world.

Were Egyptian deities all-powerful and immortal?

In hymns and prayers deities are praised for their wisdom, strength, and power. In other writings, that power seems to come with limitations. Deities were expected to obey the rules of *maat*. They might be subject to fate and they did not always know what would happen in the future. In Egyptian myth, gods were depicted as longer-lived, stronger, and more powerful than people, but they did age and they were not invulnerable. In the story known as 'The Secret Name of Ra', the sun god suffered the indignities of old age and was harmed by *heka* (magic), one of the powers he had used to make the world. That world was like a small island in the ocean of chaos, and the forces of chaos posed a continuous threat to the gods.

In their struggles with chaos monsters or with each other, Egyptian deities could be injured or even die. Such deaths rarely seem to be more than a temporary inconvenience. Isis survived being beheaded. Seth was executed in a number of unpleasant ways but always came back again. In these cases it is usually only a particular body or manifestation of the deity that dies, but Osiris seems to die in a more final manner and could not go back to his former life in Egypt. Some Underworld Books imply that the sun god died each evening and was reborn each morning. Time was made up of inescapable cycles of birth, life, death, and renewal. The creator would eventually grow weary and return into chaos until it was time for the creation of a new world.

Were Egyptian deities good?

In the majority of temple inscriptions deities seem to be gracious and generous beings. They automatically respond to prayers and offerings by heaping blessings on the king and humanity. But magical texts that offer to protect people against the very same deities suggest that all was not sweetness and light. Some divine manifestations, such as a sevenfold form of the lion goddess Sekhmet, were greatly feared. Yet Sekhmet, daughter of Ra, was not an evil goddess. The plagues and wars she inflicted were usually seen as just punishments decreed by the gods.

The 'good god' was a particular epithet of Osiris, which rather suggests that goodness was not an automatic attribute of deities. Originally the epithet may have been used as a disguised way of speaking about a terrifying death god, just as the Greeks used to refer to the dreaded Furies as 'the Kindly Ones'. In a Demotic story cycle, Osiris sends two demons to cause a civil war in Egypt and a priest-magician who discovers this divine plan is brutally murdered by Anubis.

The ethical standards expected of people do not seem to apply among the gods, but this is partly a result of turning the interaction of cosmic forces into stories with human-like characters. In myth, deities could be portrayed with human failings such as jealousy, lust, and bad temper. The earth and sky became a passionate couple (Geb and Nut) who had to be separated by force before creation could proceed. Human motivations might be provided for mythical acts, so Seth was sometimes said to attack his brother because of sexual jealousy.

Seth had many faults but his strength was needed by Ra and his inappropriate lusts could lead to beneficial results, such as the birth of a moon god. In 'The Secret Name of Ra', Isis poisons the sun god with a magic snake and will only heal him in return for the power inherent in his true name. This wicked act seems to be justified because it will culminate in her son Horus becoming the model for all kings.

In a few sources even the creator sun god seems a terrifying deity who regularly consumes all other life. Our statue group could depict both extremes of the cycle, with Sobek-Ra as the primeval deity who swallows up the world and Amonhotep III as the solar child who renews the world. However, the majority of hymns, prayers, and ethical texts do celebrate the creator as a wise and merciful being. The next chapter will look at creation myths.

Chapter 4
The beautiful moment: creation myths

The Shabaqo Stone in the British Museum has been of intense interest to Egyptologists and theologians since its inscriptions were first translated in 1901.[1] This stela is named after King Shabaqo (Shabaka) who had it made in the 8th century BC (Figure 4). The stela was retrieved from a village built over the ruins of the temple of Ptah at Memphis. For many years the basalt stela was used as a lower grindstone, so parts of its hieroglyphic inscription have been obliterated, which is ironic because the purpose of this monument was to preserve on stone the contents of an ancient worm-eaten scroll.

The text from that scroll is now known as the Memphite Theology. It is a major source for two important areas of Egyptian myth: cosmogony (creation accounts) and the mythology of Osiris. Parts of the original text seem to have been lost by the time it was copied and damage to the stone has destroyed other sections. This shows how random the survival of sources for Egyptian myth can be. It would be wrong to think that we have a complete knowledge of the subject. At any time a new discovery could overturn previous ideas.

4. The Shabaqo Stone in the British Museum

The Memphite Theology

The Memphite Theology contains not one but several creation myths. This very diversity has made the Egyptian creation story less well known than it should be. The Memphite Theology was originally dated to the early 3rd millennium BC because its language seemed to be even more archaic than that of the Pyramid Texts. Scholars interested in tracing the origins of monotheism were excited by the Memphite Theology because it seemed to provide a very early example of a transcendent deity who used the power of his intellect to create the world. Theologians lost interest in the text after it was argued that the whole thing had been written in the 8th century BC and given a false history. Most Egyptologists now believe that the creation account in the Memphite Theology was actually composed around the 13th century BC, a period when there was particular interest in creator deities. Shabaqo's scribes may have rewritten the Memphite Theology in a very archaic style to give it greater authority.

Shabaqo was a Nubian king who had forcibly reunited Egypt under his rule. His dynasty were particular worshippers of Amun-Ra as creator sun god. They revered and enriched the temples of Amun at Karnak and Ra at Heliopolis. With this stela, Shabaqo tactfully honoured the claims of Ptah and his priesthood, while promoting a text that harmonized Memphite mythology with that of Heliopolis. It is a striking example of religious and cultural sensitivity from the 8th century BC.

So, what happens in the Memphite Theology? This profound text is not easy to interpret. The inscription is a mixture of poetry and prose, third-person narrative, and speeches put in the mouths of deities. It can be divided into four main parts. The first describes how King Shabaqo restored the ancient text and gives him a divine role model in the form of Ptah-Ta-Tenen as uniter and king of Upper and Lower Egypt. The second part is similar to a surviving Middle Kingdom script for a royal ritual. It traces the history of kingship to the great debate over who should succeed the murdered god Osiris as ruler of Egypt. The first decision of Geb and the divine tribunal was to make Seth ruler of Upper Egypt, 'the place where he was born', and Horus ruler of Lower Egypt, 'the place where his father was drowned'. Their second was to unify the country by making Horus sole king.

In typical Egyptian fashion, the text then goes backwards to the death of Osiris, the father of Horus. Rather than a linear narrative, we are presented with a series of events together with their origins and consequences. These momentous events are located in and around Memphis, so that the victorious Horus can be identified with the Memphite god Ptah-Ta-Tenen. The third part of the inscription describes how Ptah created the world, while the fourth part alludes to a mystical union between Ptah and the resurrected Osiris. The cosmogony is well worth looking at in more detail.

The First Time

The Memphite Theology links Ptah with a whole series of deities who represent elements of the primeval world. These deities, 'who came into existence in Ptah', include Ptah-Nun and Ptah-Naunet, the male and female aspects of the dark, watery chaos of the primeval ocean. The potential for intelligent life was inherent in this ocean but was not realized until the spirit of the creator attained awareness. The list is damaged but it probably continued by linking Ptah with Ta-Tenen, 'the Rising Land', since elsewhere in the Memphite Theology, Ptah is identified with Ta-Tenen, the deity 'from whom everything emerged'. The rising of the first mound of land above the primeval ocean was one of the great events of the era known to the Egyptians as the 'First Time'. The mound provided a place in which the creator could come into being.

At Heliopolis, this primeval mound was associated with the sacred *ben-ben* stone, represented in temple architecture by obelisks such as Cleopatra's Needle. An alternative primal event is evoked by the

Box 6

CREATION IMAGERY

PLACES AND THINGS OF THE FIRST TIME:

Primeval ocean

Primeval marsh/reed thicket

Primeval mound

Primeval lotus

Cosmic egg

Potter's wheel

Willow tree

PRIMEVAL BEINGS:

Frogs and snakes (the Ogdoad)

Snake (Amun-Kematef, Atum, Neith)

Black bull (Amun, Ptah)

benu bird/phoenix (Atum, Ra, Osiris)

Falcon (Horus the Elder)

Goose – 'the Great Cackler' (Amun)

Ibis (Thoth)

Crocodile (Sobek-Ra, Penwenti)

Cow (Mehet-Weret, Hathor, Neith)

Sun child (Ra, Nefertem)

Moon child (Khonsu, Thoth)

Eye of Ra (Hathor, Tefnut, Bastet, Sekhmet, and others)

Hand of Atum (Hathor, Nebethetepet, Iusaas)

Seed goddess (Hathor)

The Heh gods – supporters of the sky

last deity in the list, Nefertem, 'who is at the nose of Ra'. Nefertem was the god of the primeval lotus (or water-lily). The sweet-scented blue lotus was imagined rising above the primeval ocean and opening its petals to reveal a golden child. This was 'the beautiful moment', the very first sunrise when the creator became manifest as the youthful sun god.

In creation myths from other areas, images peculiar to local deities were used to convey the unknowable beginnings of life (see Box 6). The first act of creation might be a shining bird finding somewhere to perch in the middle of the primeval ocean or a goose known as the Great Cackler laying the egg from which the sun would hatch. Egyptian cosmogonies usually list several, apparently contradictory, primal events. The Egyptians do not seem to have regarded their creation myths as literally true. They are more like highly charged metaphors, drawn from the natural world.

Creative acts

The creator was now ready to create, but what were the means of creation? Again, more than one answer to this question is given in the Memphite Theology. When speculating about the beginnings of life, the Egyptians used the models of creativity they saw around them: the sexual acts that produced people and animals, the seed-sowing that produced crops, and the powers of the mind and the hand that produced objects. Ptah was the patron deity of artists and craftsmen, but the creation account begins by linking him with Atum of Heliopolis, who created 'with his semen and his fingers'.

Passages in the Pyramid and Coffin Texts describe how Atum became lonely in the primeval ocean. He acted as both father and mother by giving himself an erection, taking his 'seed' into his mouth, and spitting out the first divine couple, Shu and Tefnut. Some versions imply that the pleasure experienced by Atum in the sexual act was a vital part of the creative process. This may seem a shockingly primitive myth, but it was illustrated in graphic detail in papyri placed in the tombs of high-ranking priests and priestesses. The androgynous nature of the creator was sometimes made clearer by personifying the hand of Atum as a goddess who united with his penis to create life.

The Memphite Theology restates the myth by using link words centred on the mouth. Atum used his mouth as a womb but the parts of the mouth could also represent the power of divine speech. The Egyptians believed that the intelligence controlling the body was located in the heart. In the Memphite Theology, Ptah is said to bring deities, people, and animals into being by devising them in his heart and naming them with his tongue. In other sources these powers of the creator are personified as the gods of insight/creative thought (Sia) and command/authoritative utterance (Hu). The 'divine words' of Ptah can, like hieroglyphs, make thoughts real. It was this more intellectual method of creation that led to comparisons between the Memphite Theology and the famous start of St John's Gospel – 'In the beginning was the Word and the Word was with God and the Word was God'.

The Memphite Theology does not deny the truth of the creation myths of Heliopolis, but it supersedes them by stating that Atum was acting as the heart and tongue of Ptah. A creation text of the Graeco-Roman Period gives Ptah a similar position in the cosmogony of Hermopolis which centred on the mysterious primeval beings collectively known as the Eight (the Ogdoad). Ptah brings the Eight into being by three means: taking thought (intellectual), fashioning eggs (craft), and fertilizing the primeval marsh with his seed (sexual). He then causes the union of the Eight which transforms them into the One: the creator god Amun.

The creation of humanity is not given any particular emphasis in the Memphite Theology. This is probably because the standard myth of the origins of humanity was firmly linked with Ra. One version has humans originate from the tears shed by the solar child when he was separated from his mother, and deities from his laughter when they were reunited. In Mesopotamian myth, humans were created as short-lived drudges to do the work of the lesser gods on earth. In Egyptian myth the creation of humanity seems more accidental, but serving the gods became a part of humanity's function.

The Memphite Theology stresses that Ptah created the moral and social order, including the concept of religion as it was to be practised by people. This primarily meant the adoration of statues which the *kas* (life-forces) of the gods would enter as bodies. Ptah also invented the crafts, such as sculpture, which humans could use to imitate his creative power. As both creator and ruler, Ptah continued as the controlling intelligence of the world like the unseen heart in the body. The gods Horus and Thoth were to embody his powers of insight and command in the age when the gods ruled Egypt.

The imperfections in the created world were not denied. The brief fourth section of the Memphite Theology reverted to the terrible tragedy of the drowning of Osiris but showed how this was transformed into something positive. Horus ensured that his father entered the secret realm where the gods of death and life could unite. The composite deity Ptah-Sokar-Osiris presided over the regeneration of the dead who were buried in the cemeteries of Memphis. In the realm of the living, the power of the creator, acting through Horus, was handed down to generations of gods and kings ruling Egypt from Memphis.

Creation myths and temples

Two German scholars who worked on early editions and translations of the Memphite Theology disagreed on what kind of text it was.[2] One thought that it was the rather garbled script of a mystery play with explanatory glosses. The other thought that it was a coherent theological treatise, though he acknowledged that the speeches it contained might derive from dramatized myths performed in temples. Creation myths were a medium for philosophical speculation, but this could be secondary to less abstract motives.

On one level, the Memphite Theology can be seen as a classic validatory myth. It justifies the continued existence of institutions such as kingship and the priesthood by giving them divine origins. When national identity is under threat from outside forces, as it was in the 8th century BC, such myths become particularly important. The public display of this creation myth to the educated elite had the effect of acknowledging the crucial importance of the temple of Ptah and its priesthood. A cynic would take the Memphite Theology as a piece of propoganda designed to lure government funding away from competing temples. This may have been one of the text's purposes, but to view it only in this way would be to overlook the transformative role of Egyptian myth.

The Memphite Theology, whether it was read aloud or inscribed on stone, was thought to have the power to influence reality for the better. Creation narratives could help to remake the world in the divine image. The passage about creation from St John's Gospel is one of the readings for Christmas Day in many Christian churches. The creation of the world and the birth of the saviour of that world are presented as parallel events. In Egyptian ritual, an account of creation is often paired with the triumph of the creator sun god, or his representative the king, over the forces of chaos. Creation myths could be set in stone without fear because they were purely positive narratives that celebrated the founding of *maat*, the divine order.

As in many other ancient cultures, creation myths were intimately bound up with the architecture and function of cult temples. In some early Egyptian temples the main feature was a mound of sand. This almost certainly represented the primeval mound where the first act of creation took place. Later temples incorporated mounds, or single obelisks, or raised the floor of the sanctuary where the god's statue was kept to above the level of the rest of the building.

Temple texts do not treat such features as symbolic reconstructions, but as the actual place of creation. The fact that most major temples made the same claim was no more disturbing to the devout than the idea that the one God can be present in the bread and wine during communion services in thousands of different churches. All sanctuaries were, in a sense, the same place.

Other creator deities

The principal deity of a temple was often equated with the creator. This meant that local deities of both genders achieved the status of creator deity. To establish this status, a creation myth might be recited or acted out during a temple festival. In the temple of Horus at Edfu, creation began with the subduing of a primeval marsh and a celestial falcon perching on a reed. In the temple of Khonsu at Karnak, Khonsu was identified with a ram-headed snake who fertilized the cosmic egg.

Where a temple had two principal deities, both could be given creation myths. At Esna the separate creative powers of the ram god Khnum and the goddess Neith were celebrated in hymns. Khnum made life with his sexual power, by releasing the Nile flood that caused crops to grow and by crafting bodies on his potter's wheel. Creation was thought of as happening both in the past and the present, since new lives continued to come into existence. Before a person could be born, Khnum or Neith had to make them a body and animate it with the breath of life.

Like Ptah in the Memphite Theology, Neith was said to use divine words to create. In some versions of her myth, only seven words of power were needed to make the world. Neith was credited with inventing childbirth. She gave birth to the sun god in her cow form, which was equated with the life-giving powers of the primeval ocean. All substances that came from the body of a deity could become life forms. The spit or vomit of Neith became the chaos monster Apophis, who was the sun god's deadliest enemy. Neith saved the solar child by lifting him above the watery chaos of the primeval ocean. As a creator, Neith seems a neutral force, making creatures of order and chaos, but by the end of the First Time she has chosen the side of order.

The sun god was often viewed as the active power of the creator in the world. In temple rituals and Underworld Books each sunset was treated like the end of the world. The nightly voyage of the sun god took him back into a dark chaotic realm. Figures from myths set in the mythical dawn of time, such as the mysterious Ogdoad and the gods of creative thought and authoritative utterance, helped the sun god to rise again and renew the world. Tomorrow was not just another day, but another world. For the Egyptians, their country was the centre of that world. In the next chapter we will look at the influence of the physical world on Egypt's mythology.

Chapter 5

Black Land, Red Land: the landscapes of myth

A set of cedarwood coffins in the British Museum is decorated with some of the oldest maps in human history (Figure 5). The coffins belonged to a doctor named Gua who lived in the 19th century BC and was buried at el-Bersheh near Hermopolis.[1] The maps claim to show the *duat*, the underworld through which the sun god and the human dead had to journey. Transected by a mighty river, this underworld contained snake-infested deserts, lakes of fire, and mysterious islands. The maps are part of a section of the Coffin Texts known as 'The Book of Two Ways'. One way through the underworld was by water (marked in blue) and the other way was by land (marked in black).

The accompanying texts describe the demons who guarded fiery gates or bends in the river; Gua was equipped with spells to get him past these fearsome guardians, including one that has him claim to be the doctor summoned to tend the wounded Osiris: 'Oh flames, make a pathway for me, so that I may come through. I restore Osiris to health.' The maps show the location of havens for the dead, such as the Field of Offerings and the Mansions of Osiris and of Thoth. Gua's ultimate goal was to join the creator sun god in his boat and sail the 'winding waterways' of earth and heaven. The mythical landscapes shown on objects like the coffin of Gua were inspired by Egypt's unique geography.

5. Floor of the outer coffin of the physician Gua

Primeval landscapes

Modern Egypt is around 90% desert, but until the 5th millennium BC the Nile Valley was one great swamp and the uplands were a vast savannah dotted with seasonal lakes. The people who became the Ancient Egyptians were hunters and cattle-herders with a semi-nomadic way of life. Outcrops of rock and conical hills that resembled the later pyramids were landmarks and gathering places. Ancient rock drawings show that the grasslands were home to a rich variety of wildlife. Many of these animals, such as the lion, the vulture, the jackal, and the gazelle, became associated with Egyptian deities.

This age of abundance did not last. A major change of climate led to the gradual drying up of the grasslands. The lack of regular rainfall made it imperative for people to find permanent sources of water. Some groups settled on the edges of the Nile Valley and ventured into the marshes among the crocodiles, cobras, hippopotami, and wild bulls. During the 4th millennium BC most people moved down into the valley. Areas of marsh were drained and cleared, and cereal farming began to be practised on a large scale. By Classical times this change was explained by the myth that Osiris had travelled among humanity, teaching them the arts of agriculture.

The river of life

The Greeks gave the Nile its name. To the Egyptians it was simply 'the river'; the only one they knew. Every year snowmelt and rainfall in the mountains of Ethiopia swelled the waters of the Blue and White Niles. They converged into a mud-filled torrent that flooded all the low-lying land within the Nile Valley and its Delta for several months. In the Delta, a few sandy hills remained permanently above the flood level. This may be why at Heliopolis and northern sites the primeval mound was said to be made of pure sand.

Box 7

THE EGYPTIAN COSMOS
The regions of the cosmos:
Outer darkness/primeval ocean

Upper sky and sky river/way of the day sun (Can be shown as
a starry sky cow or as the naked goddess Nut. The upper sky
is supported by Shu and his helpers – the Heh gods/sons of
Horus/Hathor pillars.)

Void/realm of Shu

Mountains/trees/lions of the horizon (In some images the
mouth of Nut is at the western horizon and her crotch at
the eastern horizon.)

A round earth with Egypt in the centre surrounded by
deserts and foreign lands

Duat underworld/inner sky/realm of Osiris

River of the underworld/way of the night sun (Sometimes
thought of as under the earth and sometimes as within the
body of Nut.)

Abyss/primeval ocean

Coffins like that of Gua (Figure 5) could represent the cosmos
in miniature, with a star-clock or a picture of the sky goddess
on the interior of the lid and a map of the underworld on the
floor. At certain periods Egyptian temples were designed to
symbolize the newly created cosmos. The enclosure walls
were equated with the encircling primeval ocean, the crypts
with the underworld, the pylon gateway with the mountains
of the horizon, and the roof with the upper sky.

The river dominated life for the valley-dwellers, so it was impossible for the Egyptians to conceive of a realm that had no equivalent. In Egyptian cosmology, the celestial realm in the sky and the underworld both have a river running through them (see Box 7). Other civilizations imagined the sun driving across the sky in a chariot; in Egypt, the sun, moon, and stars were shown sailing the heavens in boats. One name for Egypt was the 'Two Banks', as the river both unified and divided the country.

In many places the Nile Valley is only a few miles wide, but there were no bridges across the river. To get from one bank to the other always involved the risk of death by drowning or crocodile. The perilous boat journey became a central part of Egyptian myth. The boat of the sun god was attacked by a herd of wild asses or by the chaos serpent Apophis. The boat carrying the body of Osiris had to pass through a crowd of enemies before the god could rise again. A dead person like Gua travelled the river of the underworld using the Book of Two Ways as his guide.

The east bank of the river, where the sun rose, was the realm of the living. This made it the most appropriate site for towns and temples. The west bank, where the sun set, was designated as the realm of the dead and the proper place for cemeteries and mortuary temples. An alternative name for the underworld was the 'Beautiful West'.

Sea monsters and storm gods

The Egyptians also saw their territory as being divided into the fertile 'Black Land' of the floodplain and the barren 'Red Land' of the surrounding deserts. Osiris, Isis, and Horus were associated with the Black Land, and Seth, Nephthys, and Anubis with the Red Land. After the inundation had brought water and mud, it was possible to grow a very high yield of crops in the floodplain.

However, the precious Black Land was under constant threat from the Mediterranean Sea and from the desert.

The Mediterranean was referred to as 'the Great Green', but a more general term for the sea was 'the Encircler'. The primeval ocean, from which the creator had emerged, was still thought to surround the world. Egypt's northern coast depended on the annual deposits of silt to keep it above sea level. Coastal towns could be lost to the sea after earthquakes and tidal-waves. Land contaminated with salt was useless for cultivation. No wonder that one myth presents the sea as a greedy monster threatening to cover the whole land unless it is given more and more tribute, including the beautiful goddess Astarte. Seth, the strongest of the gods, was the champion who drove back the sea monster. This story seems to be adapted from an Ugaritic myth from Syria, but it was very relevant to the concerns of the low-lying eastern Delta, where Seth was a popular deity.

The ultimate source of the Nile was thought to be in the primeval ocean. The inundation was described as returning Egypt to its primeval state. The flood waters needed to be carefully controlled by systems of canals and dykes. When the flood levels were higher than average, villages might be swept away and people might drown. When they were lower than average, fewer crops could be grown and people might starve. The inexorable movement of the river bed could slowly destroy settlements, as seems to have happened with much of ancient Memphis.

Worship was given to the divine controllers of the Nile, such as creator gods and star goddesses, rather than the river itself. Sixteen vases or sixteen figures of Hapy, who personified the benevolent aspects of the inundation, were shown in some temples to represent the perfect water level. As time went on many core myths were reconfigured to explain the inundation and ensure its continuance. The tears that Isis shed for her murdered husband, and the substances that leaked from his body, were both said to be the cause of the inundation. The power of the inundation to bring both life and death was linked to the myth of the 'Distant Goddess'. This was the daughter of Ra who quarrelled with her father, went to live in the desert, and had to be persuaded to return.

The deserts that made up the Red Land contained valuable resources such as minerals and building stone, but expeditions sent to exploit these resources risked death through thirst, heat-exhaustion, sandstorms, or flash-floods. Land reclaimed from the desert could be overwhelmed by the violent storms said to be caused by Seth thundering in the sky, or by the slow but unstoppable progress of huge sand dunes. The need to keep irrigation canals clear of sand was so pressing that Egyptians even expected to have to do this work in the afterlife. The outer coffin of Gua is one of the earliest sources for the 'Shabti Spell' which summons a magical worker to shift sand on behalf of the deceased. Given these environmental conditions, it is not surprising that Egyptian mythology structures life as a constant struggle between the forces of order and chaos. In this struggle, all humans were expected to play their part.

Into the marshes

The myths and folk tales of many cultures involve the hero or heroine leaving their home and entering a great forest or jungle. There they can have adventures and meet supernatural beings. It is a journey of initiation and transformation. Beauty can meet the Beast, a knight can kill a dragon or find the true grail. The Egyptians had no forests or jungles, but they could leave their ordered world behind by entering a marsh or a desert.

Areas of wild marsh remained on the edges of the Nile Valley and in parts of the Delta. Marshlands were celebrated in Egyptian art and literature as places of delight and danger. They were sacred to Hathor-Sekhet, the Great Wild Cow; Sobek, Lord of Lakes; and

Wadjyt, the cobra goddess. The dead are shown in tomb paintings hunting and fishing in the domain of these deities. The tranquil reedbeds of the Delta inspired the Egyptian paradise known as the 'Field of Reeds'. It was easy to imagine that tall papyrus thickets hid the floating island of Chemmis where Isis gave birth to her marvellous son Horus. A story inscribed on the Metternich Stela tells how Isis and her seven magical scorpions fled from Seth and took refuge in a remote marsh village. She is refused hospitality by a rich woman but taken in by a fisherwoman. The scorpions sting the rich woman's child in revenge. Isis cures the child after the rich woman gives her wealth to the fisherwoman. This story probably reflects the popularity of the Delta as a hiding place for fugitives in times of political turmoil.

In an intriguing Middle Kingdom story-fragment a herdsman grazing his cattle in water-meadows encounters a goddess by a lake. Her appearence is so terrifying that the herdsman's hair stands on end and his limbs tremble, but he refuses to be driven away. In their second encounter, the goddess appears as a naked and alluring woman. Here the fragment ends, so we do not know if the herdsman accepted the goddess's erotic overtures and whether this would have been fatal. The god Seth was horribly punished for mating with a goddess he met in similar circumstances.

Beyond the valley

Equally dangerous supernatural beings were to be found just beyond the hills that edged the Nile Valley. Until around 1500 BC, the desert was shown as the home of monsters such as griffins, serpopards (snake-headed felines), and the Seth creature, which blended elements of several exotic animals. The Great Sphinx at Giza, with its lion body and human head, was a desert monster fighting on behalf of order. King Thutmose IV, the father of Amonhotep III, claimed that the sphinx had spoken to him while he slept in its shadow. The sphinx-god complained that sand had been allowed to overwhelm his body, preventing him from defending the royal tombs. The monsters become less common in art around the time when the deserts closest to Egypt were becoming more arid. As the desert lost most of its wildlife and vegetation, it became too empty to be the home of monsters.

The deep desert was the realm of the Distant, or Far-Wandering, goddess. Her story was sometimes localized to the western (Libyan) desert, the southern (Nubian) desert, or the remote land of Punt. There she roamed in the form of a wild cat, a lioness, or a female griffin. The gods who were sent to find her had to disguise themselves as apes or monkeys before they could even risk approaching her. Thoth, the god of wisdom, had to use all his eloquence to persuade this estranged daughter of Ra to leave her lonely wilderness and return to civilized society in the Nile Valley. He described how desolate Egypt was without her radiant presence and told her fables illustrating the workings of the divine order. In one, even the death of a fly is noticed by Ra and ultimately avenged by a griffin, the most terrible of the sun god's messengers.

In stories, terrifying things tended to happen to people who left Egypt. A sailor sees all his companions drown ('The Shipwrecked Sailor'); the innocent Bata is betrayed by his wife and murdered by soldiers ('The Tale of the Two Brothers'); a prince is attacked by a snake, a dog, and a crocodile ('The Doomed Prince'); a priest is robbed by pirates ('The Voyage of Wenamun'). The return of the hero to Egypt, wiser than when he left, was the proper ending for such stories. Bata manages to survive no less than three deaths to become king of Egypt.

One of the most popular of Egyptian literary texts was the story of Sinuhe. At the start of this story, Sinuhe flees from Egypt after being implicated in a plot to kill King Amenemhet I (c.1985–1956 BC). He is forced to live among the 'sand-dwellers'. Sinuhe marries the daughter of a chieftain and overcomes an enemy champion in single combat, but he longs to return home. Nothing matters more to Sinuhe than being buried in the land where he was born.

Eventually, the new king grants his wish. To an Egyptian, every part of his country was sacred ground, but many people felt a special attachment to the local deity of their home area.

Local deities and localized myths

From early times, every settlement of any size had a shrine dedicated to the god or goddess who presided over the region. In some periods, the governor of the region was also the high priest of the local deity. Eventually, each of the 42 nomes (administrative districts) of Egypt had its official deity or group of deities. The nomes were represented by a symbol or set of symbols similar to an heraldic device. These might be linked to the nome deity or to the original title of the nome. For example, the 17th Upper Egyptian nome was called the Jackal Nome; it was represented by a seated jackal with a feather, and the presiding deity was the jackal god, Anubis; whereas the 15th Upper Egyptian nome was called the Hare Nome and was represented by a hare, but the presiding deities were Thoth and the Ogdoad of Hermopolis. Gua served the governor of the Hare Nome, a man named Djehutyhotep ('Thoth is Gracious'). The Mansion of Thoth probably features in Gua's map of the underworld because Thoth was his local deity.

Local traditions were often recorded in lists of sacred beings, places, and objects. A papyrus found in Tanis lists the festivals, taboos, cemeteries, sacred animals and fish, snake-deities, sacred trees, mounds, and lakes for each nome. These lists allow a glimpse of the variety of belief beneath the uniformity imposed in temple art. In one nome it might be taboo to hunt crocodiles because they represented the benevolent god Sobek; in another it would be considered a religious act to kill them because they were 'Followers of Seth' who had fought against the good gods Osiris and Horus. In a few surviving papyri the lists are elaborated into a local mythology.

The richest source is an illustrated scroll known as Papyrus Jumilhac, which dates to around the 4th century BC. Its contents include myths that explain distinctive features of the Jackal Nome such as place names, rituals, and unusual plants, minerals, or topographical features.[2] In one section we are told that an army of the Followers of Seth had once gathered on a particular mountain. Anubis attacked them at night and severed all their heads with one blow. The mountain was covered with their blood and this was why a red mineral was still to be found in that area. This is a strictly local myth, but it forms an episode of a national one: the conflict between Horus and Seth.

Nearly all the myths in Papyrus Jumilhac are localized retellings of core myths. The riverbanks, towns, and hills of the Jackal Nome become the setting for the burial of Osiris, the defeat of Seth, and the triumph of Horus and Isis. The same cycle of myths was linked with many other areas. An Early Dynastic royal tomb at Abydos was reinterpreted during the Middle Kingdom as the burial place of Osiris. By the 1st millennium BC, Isis was said to have buried parts of the dismembered body of Osiris in every Egyptian nome. The head was supposed to be buried in Busiris in the north and one leg on the island of Biga on Egypt's southern border. Each body part represented the whole and sanctified the region.

Striking topographical features such as a mound with ancient trees, or a gap in the cliffs that resembled the fabled mountains of the horizon, might begin a mythical association, but these associations were reinforced over periods of time by ritual actions. These might range from a few words spoken during a libation to elaborate re-enactments of mythemes with a cast of thousands. Once a holy place was linked with a core myth and became a place of pilgrimage it tended to attract other associations.

These associations might be fostered by artificial manipulation of the landscape. Mounds were built to become the primeval mound or the resting place of Osiris. Lakes or pools, such as the one in which the statue of Sobek-Ra and Amenhotep III was found, were dug in temple grounds. These were used to represent the primeval ocean or the site of the watery combat between Horus and Seth. Major temples had a symbiotic relationship with the government, so royal patronage was essential for such large-scale transformations. In the next chapter we will look at the connections between royalty and myth.

Chapter 6

Lord of the Two Lands: myths of nationhood

For many people the golden mask of Tutankhamun *is* the face of Ancient Egypt. Tutankhamun's brief reign (*c.*1336–1327 BC) marked the return to an orthodox model of kingship after the 'Great Heresy' of the Amarna Period. During that period King Akhenaten had replaced all national and local mythology with accounts of the creation of the world by his solar deity, Aten. This god seemed to create and rule without opposition. The dark myths of the murder of Osiris and the bloody war between order and chaos were banished.

Tutankhamun's burial treasures allude to a wide range of myths, including those based on conflict. A pair of gilded statuettes found inside a wooden shrine show the young king standing in a shallow boat made of papyrus stems. In the statuette in the picture, Tutankhamun wears the Red Crown of Lower Egypt (Figure 6). It was the crown and other key items of royal regalia that were thought to bestow godlike powers on a king. Wearing this crown, Tutankhamun has no need of rich robes or precious jewellery to emphasize his status.

The young king holds a harpoon in one hand and a coil of rope in the other. His pose is unusually active for a royal statue – Tutankhamun is in the very act of launching his harpoon. His intended prey was a male hippopotamus but this

6. Gilded statuette of Tutankhamun as a harpooner

was a creature too dangerous to depict in the confines of the royal tomb.

The hunting of the hippopotamus

Fifteen hundred years before Tutankhamun was buried, the motif of the king as hippopotamus hunter appeared on objects belonging to Egypt's earliest kings. Hippopotamus ivory was a highly prized commodity, but hunting hippopotami with copper weapons from easily upset boats would have been a very dangerous business. A large male had to be speared many times until it had lost sufficient blood to weaken it. This was the Ancient Egyptian equivalent of a bull fight. Tradition claimed that King Menes, the legendary uniter of Egypt, had been killed by a hippopotamus.

The earliest Egyptian leaders may have had to prove their worthiness by leading such hunts, but it is highly unlikely that the frail Tutankhamun was ever allowed near a real hippopotamus. Recent research by medical historians has suggested that the young king was hardly able to stand upright without the aid of a walking-stick. At some point the hippopotamus hunt became merely symbolic. Its principal purpose could be achieved by representing it in art or through ritualized actions such as 'cutting up the hippopotamus cake'. That purpose was to bring about the triumph of order over chaos.

Many characteristics of the hippopotamus associated them with the forces of chaos. By day, hippopotami lurked just under the surface like primeval monsters in the waters of chaos. By night, they came ashore to graze, trampling crops and anything else in their path. The males fought each other ferociously. Many hippopotami are pinkish-red and red was the colour of evil in Egyptian symbolism. In myth, Seth could take the form of a hippopotamus to attack his brother Osiris or his nephew Horus, or to rebel against the sun god. It was the god Horus who hunted down the Seth-hippopotamus and stabbed him with a magic harpoon in every part of his body.

This act echoed a myth in which Horus subdued the primeval ocean with his spear so that creation could begin.

The harpooner statuette shows Tutankhamun idealized as the golden Horus-king; the hero who will slay the chaos monster and save the world. In reality the odds in such a combat were in favour of the hippopotamus, as every Nile-dweller would have known. The Egyptians did not see the triumph of order as a foregone conclusion. The threat from chaos was very real and, as with the legend of Menes, the story would not always have a happy ending. Egyptian idealogy promoted the belief that the office of kingship was essential if civilization was to survive.

King and country

It seems ironic that the men who rebelled against the British crown and established a republic in America were so fond of Ancient Egyptian symbolism, since monarchy was the keystone of Egyptian society. History was thought of in terms of lists of past kings, sometimes arranged into dynasties. These lists had the practical purpose of naming the royal ancestors who ought to be honoured with offerings. They also created a continuous history for Egypt, going back to a remote era when Egypt was ruled directly by the creator sun god and then by a series of god-kings including Osiris and Horus. The reign of Horus served as a model for all subsequent kings. All loyal subjects were to be 'Followers of Horus' rather than 'Followers of Seth'.

The deeds of several Upper Egyptian kings of the late 4th millennium BC seem to have contributed to the legend of Menes the Uniter. On royal objects of this era the king can be represented as a hawk, a bull, or a lion overcoming enemies who seem to include the 'marsh people' of the north. By around 3100 BC the world's first large nation-state had been established. Local loyalties to kin groups, tribal chieftains, or town leaders were replaced by loyalty to a central government headed by a hereditary monarchy. How was this achieved? The recent history of Africa has shown that such states cannot be sustained merely by superior force; a huge change in mental and emotional attitudes is needed.

The early kings seem to have used several methods. Firstly, they systematized writing and art to create a powerful imagery for their new country, rather as logos and trademarks are used to promote brands today. Secondly, the king entered into a relationship with all the local deities so that he became a religious leader for the whole country. Thirdly, the Egyptian elite promoted the concept of 'good authority', so that the central government was seen as part of the divine order.

The differences between north and south were celebrated rather than disguised by calling Egypt the 'Two Lands' and using paired symbols for Upper and Lower Egypt such as the White Crown and the Red Crown, the vulture and the cobra, the lily and the papyrus. Early royal annals are dominated by records of the king taking part in festivals or setting up statues in local temples. When a king celebrated his *heb sed* (jubilee festival) the gods of Upper and Lower Egypt, incarnate in their statues, gathered to validate his power.

Kings or gods?

The power of the king was based on divine authority, but were the kings themselves considered gods? Few statements about the 'divine nature' of the king would apply equally at all periods. The word *ntr* was frequently used in royal titles and statue cults were established for some living and dead kings. Coronation rituals and much of the royal regalia established the king as the earthly representative of the creator sun god who constantly renewed the world. This gave the king a position of authority in the divine hierarchy. Joseph Campbell suggested that when the Egyptian state was founded sacred kings became god-kings.[1] He argued that for much of the 3rd millennium BC 'mythic identification', in which the individuality of the king was absorbed into his sacred role, was replaced by 'mythic inflation', in which the gods were absorbed into the ego of the king.

In religious art and literature the king could take on many mythological roles, such as that of Shu supporting the sky or the child Horus being suckled in the marshes by a cow goddess. Such scenes usually pre-date representations of the gods themselves performing such actions. The statue of Tutankhamun as Horus the Harpooner is earlier than any object, such as the Metternich Stela, which shows Horus himself spearing Seth in beast form. This royal dominance seems to have been a major factor in limiting the development of narrative myths and of art illustrating myth.

From the 5th Dynasty (c.2494–2345 BC) onwards, kings used the title 'Son of Ra' (see Box 8). The king was most often presented as a loving and dutiful son to deities. He interceded with them on behalf of humanity as no one else could. One type of 'sonship' was based on ritual identification with Horus. In Egyptian religion there were essentially two deities of this name. Horus the Elder was a cosmic falcon whose eyes were the sun and the moon. Horus, son of Isis, was the royal youth who fought Seth, avenged his father Osiris, and succeeded him as ruler of Egypt. The king could be linked with both these deities but by the Middle Kingdom the most dominant formulation was living king = Horus the Younger and dead king = Osiris. The Ramesseum Dramatic Papyrus contains the script for a royal ritual re-enacting the death and resurrection of Osiris and the triumph of Horus and his sons over Seth. It is not clear whether this Middle Kingdom ritual took place as part of the coronation of the new king or the funeral of the old king.

At this period, the concept of ritual identification with deities had spread through the elite class in funerary spells like those on the coffin of Gua, and even in healing and protective magic used during daily life. This may be why a more distinctive relationship between gods and kings developed. The late Middle Kingdom story cycle in Papyrus Westcar contains an early example of a 'royal birth myth'.

Box 8

ROYAL NAMES AND TITLES

In early times kings wrote their names inside a *serekh*, a rectangle surmounted by a falcon. This identified the king as the 'Horus in the palace'. Later, kings took a series of five names when they came to the throne. The first was the 'Horus name', the second was 'the Two Ladies name', and the third the 'Golden Horus' name. The names associated with Horus demonstrated that the king was powerful and all-conquering like the god Horus. The Two Ladies were Nekhbet and Wadjyt, the tutelary goddesses of Upper and Lower Egypt. This name emphasized the unifying role of the king.

The fourth name, known as the prenomen, was written inside a cartouche and introduced by the title *nsw-bity*. This literally means 'He of the sedge and the bee', another pair of symbols for Upper and Lower Egypt. It has also been interpreted as signifying the dual aspect of the king as an individual in time and as the eternal champion of *maat*. This name often incorporates the name of Ra, as in Neb-maat-Ra, 'Ra is the lord of *maat*', the prenomen of Amenhotep III.

The fifth name, known as the nomen, is written inside a cartouche and is introduced by the phrase 'Son of Ra'. The nomen is the family name by which Egyptian kings are still known, such as Amonhotep ('Amon is Gracious'), Thutmose ('Thoth is Born'), or Tutankhamun ('Living image of Amun'). These names sometimes reflect a dynasty's allegiance to the local god of their place of origin. For example, the family of Seti I ('He of Seth') is known to have come from a part of the eastern Delta where the cult of Seth was prominent.

The first three rulers of the 5th Dynasty are said to be the sons of Ra by a human woman. Their miraculous birth is attended by the divine sisters Isis and Nephthys, the frog-goddess Heqet, and the birth goddess, Meskhenet. The god Khnum gives health to each of the triplets as they are born.

Khnum was supposed to fashion each person's body and *ka*, a kind of vital force, on his potter's wheel. He is shown doing this in New Kingdom temple scenes illustrating the divine conception and birth of rulers. Reliefs in Luxor temple show Amun-Ra, King of the Gods, visiting a queen to beget a marvellous child who will reign as Amenhotep III (see Figure 3). When Amenhotep is born the deities who protected the solar child and the infant Horus gather to honour the baby prince and his mother.

The royal *ka* seems to have been regarded as an immortal power that dwelt in the body of each king, rather as the *ka* of a deity was thought to dwell in a cult statue. The term *ka* may derive from the Egyptian word for 'nourishment'. It also sounded like the word for 'bull' and connections of this kind were thought to be significant. The *ka* of the king sustained all his subjects. Each king was said to become the 'Bull of his Mother' in order to beget another form of himself who would succeed as the next king and the eternal champion of order.

Order versus chaos

A king was supposed to establish *maat* on earth by building temples, making offerings to the gods and the spirits of the dead, giving justice to the living, and defending the borders of Egypt. One text specifies that the role of the king was 'to put *maat* in the place of *isfet* (chaos)'. This implies that *isfet* was thought of as the natural state of affairs. The forces of chaos that the king had to subdue could be represented in iconography by foreigners, flocks of migratory birds, or various desert and marsh animals, such as the oryx and the hippopotamus. The harpooner statuette shows a uraeus (a coiled cobra) attached to the king's crown. This fire-spitting cobra goddess was held to be the constant companion of every legitimate king. In myth, she was the lost eye of Ra who returned to the brow of the sun god and took on snake form to defeat his enemies.

Chaos was not presented as totally evil. Beings such as Nun, god of the chaotic primeval ocean, were honoured as 'fathers' of the creator. It is implied that some elements of chaos were neccessary for survival and had to be harnessed rather than eliminated. The energy and strength of the chaos god Seth were needed when the forces of order faced monsters such as the insatiable sea or the serpent Apophis. People were thought to have the capacity to choose between living in *maat* or *isfet*. In a spell in the Book of Two Ways (Coffin Text 1130) the creator states that he commanded people to do no wrong but their hearts disobeyed him. Like the creator, people had the power to make their own reality through what they thought. In the myth of 'The Destruction of Humanity' death comes into being because people rebel against the authority of 'King Ra'. Allusions to the dire consequences of rebellions against good authority are found throughout Egyptian literature.

A Middle Kingdom text known as the 'Loyalist Instruction' assigned two mythological roles to the reigning king: that of the creator sun god who gave light, water, and air to humanity, and that of the terrible lion goddess who devoured the enemies of order. This cross-gender identification is not as startling as it sounds since the lion goddess was a manifestation of the eye goddess who was originally part of the sun god. The Loyalist Instruction argued that strict organization was needed to defend the country, to exploit the inundation, and to grow enough food to allow the practice of crafts. The benefits of peace and prosperity were offered in return for the loss of individual or local freedoms. The elite class who helped the king to govern took a larger share of this prosperity than anyone else and so had a vested interest in continuing the system.

Nevertheless, some of the literature produced by and for this elite class is surprisingly critical of individual kings.

Kings behaving badly

In literature, it can be honest officials or learned priests and magicians who embody good authority rather than the king. Surviving Egyptian tales paint an unflattering picture of royal behaviour. In Papyrus Westcar, King Khufu gets rebuked by a peasant-magician for wanting to experiment on people. In the 'Tale of King Neferkare and Sasanet' the king has an illicit affair with a general. In Papyrus Vandier a king sacrifices a loyal subject to save himself and then seizes the dead man's wife and goods. In the 'Tale of the Two Brothers' a king steals another man's wife and allows his new queen to slaughter a sacred bull.

Classical writers who visited Egypt recounted even worse tales about ancient kings who raped their daughters or forced them to work as prostitutes in order to finance their building works. Some of these instances may arise because mythemes have been transposed into the human world, but it does appear that the Egyptians made a sharp distinction between the sanctity of the office and the fallibility of individual holders of that office. The same attitude seems to apply in narratives in which deities reign as kings and queens of Egypt.

The gods themselves are treated as existing in two types of time: a continuous present that can be accessed by ritual and in a remote past when the world was different. In the former, the gods are powerful cosmic forces whose interactions are not governed by petty human concerns. In the latter deities can appear as fallible beings with desires and emotions. In the myth of 'The Secret Name of Ra', the sun god is poisoned by Isis and tricked into giving her power over him. In 'The Destruction of Humanity' King Ra vacillates about what to do with rebellious humanity and is too distressed to remain on earth. In both these myths Ra asks a council of gods for advice, just as an Egyptian king was expected to listen to his councillors' advice before choosing a course of action.

In a myth recorded in the late 1st millennium BC, the god Geb is burned by the cobra goddess on the crown after driving his father King Shu into exile and forcing his mother Tefnut to become his queen. The arcane doctrine of the 'Bull of his Mother' has been taken literally and turned into a story of incest and filial rebellion. The harpooner statuette of Tutankhamun illustrates an episode in another myth centred on the royal succession: the conflict between Horus and Seth over who should be king. For 3,000 years this was the primary national myth of Egypt. The reigning king was more closely identified with Horus than with any other deity, yet many different resolutions to the conflict are recorded. In the next chapter we will look in detail at one version of this myth and the diverse ways in which it has been interpreted.

Chapter 7

The big fight: conflict and reconciliation

Among the treasures of the Chester Beatty Library in Dublin is Papyrus Chester Beatty I. This papyrus scroll contains a number of literary works in poetry and prose, including a mythological narrative known as 'The Contendings of Horus and Seth' (Figure 7). The scroll was once part of a private library that belonged to a family who lived and worked in the royal necropolis of Western Thebes during the late New Kingdom. The Contendings is in the same hieratic handwriting as another text in Papyrus Chester Beatty I: a hymn to celebrate the accession of King Ramesses V (*c.*1156–1151 BC). The scribe who wrote out these two texts may also have composed them. Most of the incidents in the Contendings can be traced to earlier sources, but no other version of the myth combines them in the same way.

The Contendings is one of the longest narratives to survive from Ancient Egypt. It is also one of the most controversial. The text has been viewed as a crude entertainment, a clever satire, a sophisticated fiction, or a transformative myth. The Contendings has been used to shed light on the inauguration ceremonies of Egyptian kings, the unification of Egypt, the rise of royal power in the Middle Kingdom, the decline of royal authority in the late New Kingdom, gender issues, and the workings of the Egyptian legal system. It has been analysed, with diverse results, by Freudians,

7. Page from the story of 'The Contendings of Horus and Seth' in Papyrus Chester Beatty I

structuralists, and poststructuralists. These multiple interpretations of the Contendings show that there is no one standard reading of any Egyptian myth.[1]

A shocking story

Religious texts were normally composed in classic Middle Egyptian, but the Contendings is largely written in the colloquial language of the late New Kingdom. The deities in the story often speak in an informal way rather than in the flowery language of temple inscriptions. Nor do the protagonists behave in the decorous manner of deities in temple reliefs. In this version of Egypt's national myth, the sun god cannot make up his mind to do the right thing and sulks when contradicted; Horus, the model for all kings, cheats to win a contest and beheads his mother in a fit of temper; while Seth, the patron deity of some New Kingdom rulers, figures as a violent and lustful buffoon (see the summary in Box 9).

In the introduction to his translation of the Contendings, E. F. Wente argued that, 'The behaviour of some of the great gods is at points so shocking that it is hard to imagine that no humor was intended'.[2] Some scholars believe that the humorous element disqualifies the Contendings from being a myth and makes it mere entertainment; others have pointed out that providing meaningful entertainment is an important function of myths in many cultures.

Modern readers of the Contendings might assume that educated people in Western Thebes had ceased to believe in their deities, but there is plenty of archeological evidence to refute such an idea. Scribes who worked in the necropolis set up household altars, built and ran community shrines, participated in religious festivals, and decorated their own tombs with scenes of gods. It is most likely that any criticism in the text is aimed at the king and his representatives who chose to identify themselves with the sun god and his council of

Box 9

SUMMARY OF 'THE CONTENDINGS OF HORUS AND SETH'

Horus and Seth have been disturbing all Egypt with their quarrel over who should be king. The youthful Horus appears before a tribunal of deities to claim the throne of his dead father, Osiris. Several gods proclaim that Horus is in the right, but the All-Lord (creator sun god) is annoyed that the tribunal is making a decision without consulting him. Seth demands that the question be settled by single combat. Thoth writes a letter to Neith, asking for her advice. She writes back threatening to send the sky crashing to the ground if the throne isn't given to Horus. The tribunal agrees with Neith, but this makes the sun god furious. The sun god tells Horus that he is just a feeble boy, unfit to be a king. This makes the other gods angry and one of them insults the sun god.

The sun god is very upset. He lies down in his tent and refuses to get up until his daughter Hathor displays her genitals to him. Then the sun god tells Horus and Seth to speak for themselves. Seth argues that he should be king because he is the only god strong enough to defend the sun god from the chaos serpent who attacks him every day. The sun god wishes to give the throne to Seth, but other gods complain that Horus has a better claim. Isis becomes very angry and the gods try to pacify her. This in turn makes Seth angry. He threatens to kill one god each day unless Isis is banned from the tribunal.

The gods agree to meet on an island in the river. They order the divine ferryman, Nemty, not to ferry Isis to the island. Isis disguises herself as an old woman and bribes Nemty with a gold ring. Once on the island she transforms herself into a beautiful young woman so that Seth will desire her. She spins Seth a sad story about how a stranger has deprived her young son of his cattle (which in Egyptian sounds like the word for inheritance). When Seth declares that this is infamous, Isis tells Seth that he has judged himself guilty. The other gods agree, but they do give in to Seth's demand that Nemty be horribly punished.

The morning and evening forms of the sun god declare that Horus should be crowned king, but Seth won't accept the verdict. He challenges Horus to a competition. They will both take the form of hippopotami and see who can stay submerged longest. Isis fears that Horus will drown, so she tries to spear Seth with her magic harpoon. First she hits Horus. When she harpoons Seth, he reminds her that they are brother and sister, and she lets him go. Horus leaps out of the water and beheads her. The sun god has Thoth heal Isis and orders that Horus be punished. Seth finds Horus sleeping and tears out and buries both of his eyes. Hathor discovers the blinded Horus and restores his eyes with gazelle milk. The buried eyes grow into lotuses.

The gods tell Horus and Seth to make peace and Seth invites Horus to stay in his house. During the night Seth tries to establish dominance by having sex with Horus, but Horus catches Seth's semen in his hand. He tells Isis, who cuts off his polluted hand and makes him a new one. Then she rubs the penis of Horus, gathers some of his semen and spreads it on the lettuce plants in Seth's garden. When Seth eats the lettuces he becomes pregnant by Horus. In front of the tribunal Seth mocks Horus for submitting to him. Horus responds by telling Thoth to call to his own and Seth's semen and see where it answers from. Seth's semen answers from the water but the semen of Horus answers from inside Seth. Thoth summons the semen of Horus. It emerges from the head of Seth as a shining disc which Thoth places on his own head.

The tribunal declare that Horus is in the right, but Seth demands another contest: a race in boats made of stone. Seth makes a huge boat out of a mountaintop, but Horus makes his boat out of wood, painted to look like stone. The stone boat sinks, so Seth turns into a hippopotamus and attacks the other boat. Horus harpoons the Seth hippopotamus but the other gods tell him to stop. Horus sails to Sais to complain to Neith that justice still has not been done.

Thoth suggests that the tribunal write a letter to Osiris in the underworld asking for his opinion. When Osiris reads the letter he demands to know why Horus has been cheated of his birthright. Osiris reminds the tribunal that he was the one who sustained the world by creating barley and emmer wheat. The sun god responds that crops would have grown even if Osiris had never existed. This enrages Osiris. He sends a letter accusing the sun god of creating injustice. Osiris points out that the demons of the underworld do not fear any god or goddess and can fetch the hearts of all wrongdoers to face judgement. The gods acknowledge that this is true. Atum tells Isis to bring Seth to the tribunal in chains.

When Seth is made prisoner, he agrees that Horus should be king. Isis shouts with joy when her son is crowned. The sun god takes Seth to live with him in the sky as god of thunder storms. Heaven and earth rejoice to see Horus arise as king.

advisory deities. Horus's complaint that he has been struggling
to obtain justice for 80 years would surely have struck a chord
with the original audience, since some legal cases in Thebes
are known to have dragged on for many years. Disputes about
inheritances were common and surviving legal documents
show how hard it was for widows and orphans (such as Isis
and Horus) to obtain their rights even when the law was on
their side.

The most shocking incidents in the story, such as the beheading of
Isis or the pregnancy of Seth, are duplicated in some other sources,
such as magical texts and calendars linking days to mythical events.
Seth's attempted seduction or rape of his nephew Horus was a
popular theme in Egyptian literature for over 2,000 years. The
author of the Contendings displays a very wide-ranging knowledge
of Egyptian myth, including localized myths of the kind later
recorded in Papyrus Jumilhac.

Origins of a conflict

In the 19th century AD there were several main schools of thought
about the origins of myths. Myths were seen as descriptions of
forces of nature or of the movements of heavenly bodies; as
garbled or romanticized history; or as evolving to explain archaic
rituals. In the 20th century AD, myths were interpreted as
reflecting aspects of the human mind and its ability to make sense
of the world and to formulate language. All of these theories have
been used at one time or another to explain the enmity between
Horus and Seth.

In the early stages of Egyptian religion, Horus seems to have been
worshipped as a sky god. The evidence for Seth as a god of sand and
rain storms appears somewhat later, but it has led some scholars to
see Horus and Seth as opposing forces of nature. The mytheme of
Seth's theft of the eye of Horus has often been interpreted as an
explanation of a lunar eclipse. The Egyptians certainly identified

Horus, or his eyes, with a variety of heavenly bodies such as the noon-day sun, the full moon, and the morning star. The theory that astronomical observations had a formative influence on Egyptian myth is currently popular.

The idea that myths transformed historical people into deities goes back to the Ancient Greeks. Plato, for example, assumed that the god Thoth had been a real person of the remote past. This theory has few contemporary adherents and is rarely proposed by Egyptologists for deities other than Horus and Seth. Recent archaeological evidence has been used to suggest that the Horus and Seth myth might have its origins in a conflict between the rulers of Nagada (local deity Seth) and Hierakonpolis (local deity Horus) in the late 4th millennium BC.[3] This is not to say that Horus and Seth were based on particular historical figures, only that a war fought in their names might have shaped the myths told about these deities.

Myth and history

The conflict between Horus and Seth was continually re-imagined in response to differing political situations. In most 2nd millennium BC versions of the myth, the emphasis is on ending the conflict through mediation. Peace is established when the 'Two Lords' are each given a realm to rule – the Black Land for Horus and the Red Land for Seth. Then the two gods will unite their strength to support the divine order. This seems to reflect a pragmatic approach to settling civil strife. However, after Egypt suffered a devastating series of invasions and occupations in the 1st millennium BC, the emphasis changed and the desired end of the conflict was usually the brutal execution of Seth and the annihilation of his followers.

The particular version recorded in the Contendings may have been influenced by, or even have been a commentary on, the troubled royal succession during the 12th century BC. Only a few years before the story was written down, a prince who was the son of a queen called Isis had managed to gain the throne in spite of a murderous plot by one of his brothers. The Encomium in Papyrus Chester Beatty I acclaims Ramesses V as a Horus who has succeeded his father Osiris, but there is some evidence that his succession led to a civil war with his brother or nephew, Ramesses VI. The lives of the royal tomb-builders could be severely disrupted by such conflicts. They were bound to hope for a peaceful resolution to a succession crisis, such as the final division of power in the Contendings.

One Egyptologist has suggested that both the Encomium and the Contendings were composed to be recited during a festival at Thebes to celebrate the accession of Ramesses V.[4] The existence of the Ramesseum Dramatic Papyrus shows that validating kingship was a definite function of the Horus and Seth myth. Was royal ritual also its origin, or was the myth usurped by royalty to suit their own purposes? When asking which comes first, the myth or the ritual, each case has to be judged on its own merits. Often existing rituals, such as funerary rites, seem to have been gradually enhanced through association with myths.

Learning from myth

Many scholars have seen myth and ritual as virtually interchangeable, with myth as the 'thing spoken' and ritual as the 'thing done'. Claude Lévi-Strauss, the founder of structuralism, a method of interpreting and analysing aspects of culture and human experience, took a different view. He argued that while myths confront the universal problems and irreconcilable conflicts of the human condition, rituals gloss over them as though they do not exist. The royal and funerary rituals that incorporate elements of the Horus and Seth myth do seem to deny the reality of death and discord. In ritual, the new king is always Horus, the loving son, succeeding his father Osiris. By contrast, in the Contendings it proves almost impossible to choose between Horus and Seth, who seem to represent paired but opposing concepts, such as culture and nature. The structuralist Robert Oden notes that 'there are binary oppositions with a vengence' in the Contendings. He argues that the structure of the tale articulates these oppositions without attempting to reconcile them. If so, this stands in contrast to many religious treatments of the Horus and Seth myth.

Freudians, who link myths to infantile sexual fantasies that shape the psyche, can find plenty to work with in the Contendings. Horus has to deal with a distant and passive father figure (Osiris), a violent and sexually abusive father figure (Seth), and a desired but domineering mother (Isis). In some versions, Horus establishes dominance by raping Isis rather than beheading her. The crowning of Horus could be interpreted as the adolescent Horus achieving maturity. Carl Jung saw Osiris as the part of the ego that had to give way or change in order for individuation to take place. In Jung's writings on Egyptian myth, Horus is variously said to represent light, humanity, the dawn of consciousness, and the perfected self.

Such psychoanalytical approaches can make ancient myths meaningful for modern people, but would they have had any validity for Egyptians of the 12th century BC? Like structuralism, these analyses ignore the known functions of a particular text, such as validating kingship, and the relationship of the myth being interpreted to the 'mythical history' of the culture in question. Interpreting the Contendings only in terms of family dynamics wrenches events from their setting. For example, the sexual nature of the relationship between Isis and Horus looks different if it is seen as part of a sequence of repeating mythical events.

The basic mytheme is 'goddess arouses god in order to create life'. When the murdered Osiris entered an inert state, Isis used her magic to sexually arouse him and conceive Horus. In some creation myths, the Hand Goddess aroused the penis of the primeval form of the sun god so that the first deities could be conceived and creation could begin. The means of creation could also involve the creator fertilizing a plant, such as the primeval lotus or reed bed, with his 'seed'. In the Contendings, a lettuce is fertilized after Isis arouses Horus. This results in the birth of a solar disc, as in the first sunrise of creation. Everything that comes from the body of Horus, including his eyes, is capable of creating life. It marks him as the true heir of the creator sun god.

This is not to deny that basic truths about the human mind may have shaped the Horus and Seth myth. The Egyptians did interpret events symbolically, and there is even some evidence that they used their mythology to illuminate human behaviour. A New Kingdom text that comes from the same private library as Papyrus Chester Beatty I divides men into Followers of Seth and Followers of Horus. The 'Seth man' is characterized as hot-tempered, lustful, and over-emotional. The 'Horus man', on the other hand, has presumably learned to control his desires and emotions in order to act effectively. The text continues with a list of dream interpretations based on the 'personality type' of the dreamer.

The triumph of Horus

Acknowledging that the Egyptians used their mythology in sophisticated ways, the Egyptologist Michèle Broze has treated the Contendings as a subtle work of literature. She has pointed out that rather than being pointlessly repetitive, the text is structured by paired events that gradually establish the claim of Horus. There are two coronation scenes, one aborted and one successful; two deities (Neith and Osiris) are consulted like oracles; Isis undergoes two sets of transformations; the goddess Hathor reactivates two deities (the sun god and Horus). The two fights involving hippopotami form an interesting example of paired events with negative and positive values.

In the first incident, a kind of trial by ordeal, both deities take the form of a hippopotamus and plunge into the sea. When Horus becomes a creature associated with destruction and enters the waters of chaos, he takes on chaotic qualities. He falls into a destructive rage, beheads his mother, a crime against the natural order of things, and fails to prove his case. In the second combat, only Seth is in hippopotamus form and Horus harpoons him from a boat. This would evoke the traditional image of the king as the champion of order defeating chaos, as in the harpooner statuette of Tutankhamun (Figure 6). From this point in the story, Horus's claim to be king is obviously justified.

This single text is so rich in interest that whole books have been written about it. The Contendings of Horus and Seth can stand on its own as an enjoyable tale, but it is far more meaningful when seen as part of Egyptian mythology as a whole. A particular quality of Egyptian myth is the way that everything interlocks. In the next chapter we will look at how the myths interacted with each other and how a single image could come to stand for a whole complex of myths.

Chapter 8
The eyes of heaven: pairs and sequences

The two most important elements in Egyptian religion, the solar cult and the Osiris cult, are brought together in the single image of the 'sacred eye'. Kings were buried wearing pairs of sacred eye bracelets. The incision wound on elite mummies was often covered with a metal plate bearing a sacred eye. In life and death ordinary people wore sacred eye amulets, such as the ones in Figure 8. The sacred eye spread from Egypt to other cultures and is one of the best known of Ancient Egyptian symbols today. A version of it is used by the American Association of Pharmacists as the emblem of their profession.

8. Three amulets representing lunar and solar eyes

The eye in the sky

The sacred eye contains elements of a human eye combined with the markings of a falcon. It is often referred to as the 'eye of Horus', the falcon god. Readers who have got this far will be unsurprised to learn that things are not as simple as that. For a start, Horus has more than one eye. When Horus is considered as a cosmic being, his right eye is equated with the sun or the morning star and his left eye with the moon or the evening star. The sun disc was also worshipped as the active power of Ra in the world, an all-seeing eye in the sky.

Many Egyptian goddesses, such as Tefnut, Hathor, Mut, Sekhmet, and Bastet, could take the role of the 'eye of Ra who defends her father Ra'. Like the eye of Horus, the eye of Ra could function separately and have mythical adventures on its own. When the eye of Ra returned to her father, he placed her on his forehead as the fire-spitting cobra who would defeat his enemies. She is the cobra we see on the crowns worn by Sobek-Ra and Amenhotep III (Figure 3) and Tutankhamun (Figure 6).

The eyes of Horus and the eye of Ra could all be shown as a sacred eye. It is sometimes possible to identify a sacred eye amulet as either solar or lunar, according to whether it is left- or right-facing, by the material used, or by details added to the basic eye. The amulet in the middle of Figure 8 is clearly the solar eye because it is made from bright red carnelian and incorporates a cobra crowned with a solar disc – two forms of the eye of Ra.

As amulets, the lunar Horus eye basically stood for healing and wholeness, and the solar Ra eye for power and protection. In some contexts both qualities might be required. For example, sacred eye amulets were placed on a mummy to make it whole and to protect it from harmful forces. These simple meanings derive from a number of myths that gradually developed ever closer and more complex connections. According to temperament, people find the connectivity of Egyptian myth fascinating or infuriating. Readers who think that they might fall into the latter category should omit this chapter.

Ways of myth-making

Egyptian myths were not all generated at the dawn of history and handed down unchanged. Myth-making was a continuous process. There must have been generally understood rules governing this process, as there were for the creation of religious art. Important methods for bringing originally diverse elements together were 'word-linkage' and the arrangement of deities into family groups. We have already seen these used to merge creation myths in the Memphite Theology in Chapter 4. Through syncretism, the myths originally attached to one deity could be transferred to their divine 'partner', as with Ra and Sobek.

A fourth mechanism for change and development was to invent or adapt a mytheme so that it formed a pair with an existing mytheme or could be fitted into an existing sequence of parallel events. This allowed myths to be created specially to fulfil a variety of public and private functions. One example is the sequence based on the mytheme 'goddess arouses inert god' that we looked at in Chapter 7. Another is the series of divine children born from the era of creation down to historical times. The solar child was born in the primeval lotus and protected by the primeval cow; the Horus child was born in the papyrus thicket of Chemmis and protected by the wild cow of the marshes; rulers such as Amenhotep III were born through divine intervention and were shown being nursed by cow goddesses.

In the daily solar cycle, the sun could be thought of as a child emerging from the primeval waters or born to the cow goddess every morning. The solar child was important from early times, but the matching concept of a lunar child, who is also shown emerging from a lotus, does not seem to have been introduced until the end of the New Kingdom. This kind of repetition was not just a literary device, it reflected the way that Egyptian intellectuals thought about time and causality.

History repeats itself

According to one Egyptian text, 'Everything that exists is eternal stability and eternal recurrence'. Paradoxically, stability was achieved by regular changes or transformations. Kingship, for example, was an eternal part of the divine order, but it functioned through a recurring pattern of the old king dying and becoming Osiris and the new king taking his place as Horus. Terrible events such as murder and rebellion were part of the pattern because of the continuing presence of chaos, but they would be balanced by the positive transformations that allowed the world to be renewed. As on the Metternich Stela, the divine child was always under threat but would always survive to triumph over the enemies of order.

Time could be thought of as going all the way back to the First Time like a straight line, and as going round in circles as key events repeated themselves in hourly, daily, monthly, or annual cycles. Egyptian creation texts, such as the Memphite Theology, are like personal timelines for creator deities. The most humanized mythical narratives belong to the remote period when the earth was directly ruled by a series of deities. Since they were set in the past their influence on the present was limited. When similar events recurred in works based on cyclical time, they were mainly expressed through images and the bringing together of 'constellations' of deities. Turning the solar cycle into too human or too specific a story might damage its power of 'eternal recurrence' and with it the whole workings of the universe. Nevertheless, it is possible to observe a long, slow process of link-building between the solar cycle and other elements of Egyptian myth. Looking at a few more examples of pairs and sequences may make this clearer.

Paired mythemes

I have listed eight pairs of mythemes involving divine eyes, or the heavenly bodies which can be associated with such eyes (see Box 10). To call these pairs alternative versions of a single myth would not be accurate. This is not a case of something happening *either* one way or another. It has, or will have, happened *both* ways.

The pattern for all future events was set during the First Time, the period when the universe was being created, so pairs often consist of an event that happened during the First Time and an event that is placed during the era when deities ruled the earth (as in pairs 1–2). In other pairs, one event seems to take place in linear time and the other in cyclical time (for example, pair 7). In the daily solar cycle, dawn is equivalent to the First Time and evening to the end of mythical history when the creator returns to chaos. Events set very early in mythical history often seem to have been invented quite late in Egypt's cultural history, since the peak of interest in the First Time, and the chaos that preceded it, was during the 1st millennium BC.

There are two main kinds of paired mythemes, which could be labelled symmetrical and non-symmetrical. When reduced to essentials, symmetrical pairs are identical events with different protagonists. For example, the summary 'deity loses his eye and gets it back', would apply to both Ra and Horus (pair 3). In non-symmetrical pairs at least one element is reversed, thus the eye of Ra is the means of both the creation and the destruction of humanity (pair 1). Each myth in a pair is enriched by knowledge of the other. Horus's role as an avatar of the sun god is made clear by the loss and return of his life-giving eye. Humanity's origin in tears of anger and sorrow foreshadows its eventual fate.

Once a pairing was established, there was often a transfer of imagery or actors between the two myths. From very early times,

Box 10

PAIRED EYE MYTHS

1
Humanity springs from tears of eye of the Ra-Atum
Humanity is destroyed by the eye of Ra

2
Eye of Ra retrieves Shu (and Tefnut) from primeval waters
Shu retrieves eye of Ra (Hathor-Tefnut) from distant desert

3
Ra loses his eye and regains it
Horus loses his eye and regains it

4
Thoth (or Shu) heals and returns the lost eye of Horus
Shu (or Thoth) transforms and returns the strayed eye of Ra

5
Ra reinvigorated by return of eye of Ra
Osiris regenerated through presentation of eye of Horus

6
Seth as black boar swallows eye of Horus (moon)
Nut, 'the sow', swallows the sun disc (eye of Ra)

7
Seth 'gives birth' to the solar or lunar disc
Nut gives birth to the sun in the morning

8
Seth tears out the eye or eyes of Horus
Horus tears off the testicles of Seth

the conciliatory god Thoth was credited with restoring the eye of Horus. In the original myth of the return of the Distant Goddess, the god who brought her back seems to have been Onuris or Onuris-Shu. Once this goddess became identified with the lost eye of Ra, symmetry demanded that Thoth become her chief restorer. Thoth was said to have adopted his baboon form to approach and pacify the angry goddess. By the end of the Middle Kingdom, an image of a baboon holding out a sacred eye could represent one or both of these mythemes. Later still, Shu was sometimes named as the god who had retrieved the eye of Horus from the hand of Seth.

Thoth's baboon form was particularly associated with his role as a moon god. Sacred eye amulets decorated with tiny troops of monkeys or baboons (for example, Figure 8, right) could evoke this lunar aspect and/or the narrative motif of the eye goddess escorted back to Egypt by deities in baboon form and welcomed by monkeys and other animals. The apes create a further visual link with the traditional image of the newly risen sun adored by a troop of baboons (see Figure 2a). When the lost eye returns, Osiris rises from the dead and the sun rises to drive away darkness.

Parallel events

The same mytheme can be part of several pairs or sequences. Its emphasis will change according to the other elements present. For example, Thoth returning the eye goddess to Ra can be paired with Thoth bringing Ra's gentle daughter Maat to join the sun god. The presentation of Maat to Ra can also be equated with the presentation of the eye of Horus to Osiris. In both cases, a god receives something that he needs in order to function. This is a literary equivalent to the varied deployment of symbols in works of art such as royal jewellery.

The paired mytheme 'deity loses eye and gets it back' can also form part of a long sequence of mutilations of deities (see Box 11). Mutilation was a fate particularly dreaded by Egyptians because

Box 11

MUTILATIONS SEQUENCE

Seth dismembers body of Osiris – body restored by Isis and Anubis

Seth tears apart eye of Horus – eye restored by Thoth

Seth tears out both eyes of Horus – eyes restored by Hathor or Isis

Horus tears off the testicles of Seth – testicles restored by Thoth

Horus beheads Isis – Thoth gives Isis a cow's head

Isis cuts off the hand/hands of Horus – Isis makes him new ones, or hands recovered by Sobek

Horus, Anubis, or Isis castrate and dismember Seth

Seth, Horus, and others mutilate Apophis and the Enemies of Ra

killing someone by beheading or dismemberment was thought to restrict their power in the afterlife. A standard way of punishing dead people and rendering them harmless was to destroy the eyes of their tomb statues or erase their faces in tomb paintings.

The most famous mutilation in Egyptian myth was the wounding of the eye or eyes of Horus. He was sometimes worshipped as a pair of deities, the benevolent Horus-with-eyes and the vengeful Horus-without-eyes. Like other terrible and inauspicious events, the mutilation of Horus is never directly shown in art and is rarely described in detail in literature. Seth always seems to be the perpetrator. Sometimes he is said to damage or rip the eyeball or pupil of Horus out with his finger. In the Contendings, Seth tears out both eyes and buries them in a secret place. Sometimes Seth is said to swallow the eye of Horus. In a few texts, the eye appears to be lost in the dark primeval ocean, a fate that may be borrowed from the paired myth of the lost eye of Ra-Atum. To remove the divine eye is to remove light and hope and plunge the world into despair and darkness.

It became axiomatic that the eye of Horus was not just lost but divided into many pieces. In the lunar calendars used by temples the loss and restoration of the eye of Horus was equated with the waning and the waxing of the moon. Thoth was the deity usually given the role of putting the eye back together, even though one part remained missing. Through the magic of Thoth, the wounded eye of Horus became the *wedjat* (the complete or sound eye). The elements of the sacred eye could be used in the hieroglyphic script to write fractions: the pupil writing 1/4, the eyebrow 1/8, and so on. The parts of the eye add up to 63/64, with the missing part magically added by Thoth. These fractions were most often employed to measure grain, or the relative proportions of drugs to be used in medicinal prescriptions.

At some point, the story of the fate of the body of Osiris seems to have been manipulated to make it more similar to the fate of the eye of Horus. Originally, Isis had to search for the decomposed body of Osiris and restore it with her magic. Then the idea developed that Seth had ripped the body apart and scattered the pieces. Eventually, as we saw in Chapter 5, there was one body part for each of the 42 nomes of Egypt. Isis gathered the fragments, using magic to make a replacement for the one body part that remained missing.

The intact eye of Horus had the power to heal the living, bestow kingship, and make the dead whole again. The intact body of Osiris was credited with the power to make the Nile rise and the crops grow. The mutilations of Horus and Osiris seem to lead to increased power. Even the beheading of Isis had a positive result when she acquired the powers of the cow goddess with her new cow head. These mutilations seem like a violent version of the voluntary transformations the sun god underwent during his daily voyage through the skies above and below the earth.

The case of the mutilation of Seth is rather different. In the oldest sources (in which Seth and Horus are generally regarded as brothers rather than uncle and nephew), two pairs of life-giving circular objects, the eyes of Horus and the testicles of Seth, are damaged. Thoth has to heal both wounds so that the equilibrium can be restored. Then Seth, strongest of the gods, will join Horus the Harpooner, the eye of Ra, and many other warlike deities to defeat and dismember the ultimate enemy, the chaos serpent Apophis. This fits the pattern of mutilations as ultimately beneficial transformations. Later sources usually have Seth mutilated as a punishment for his crimes without any subsequent healing or making whole.

Papyrus Jumilhac contains several stories about the eyes of Horus and the body of Osiris localized to the Jackal Nome. In one, Seth is punished by Anubis for trying to tamper with the body of Osiris. The flesh of Seth is roasted so that the aroma reaches Ra in the sky. The skin of Seth in his panther form is cut off, branded, and worn as a cloak by Anubis. This myth provided an explanation for priests wearing leopard-skin cloaks during funerary rituals. By the Graeco-Roman Period, the body of Seth was said to have been divided into many parts after his defeat. One part was buried in each of the 42 nomes, forming negative counterparts to the body parts of Osiris.

Popular tales

The theme of mutilation is also found in some popular tales. In one New Kingdom story, a younger brother is jealous of his elder sibling, just as Seth was jealous of Osiris. The names of these two brothers, Maat and Gereg, are usually translated as Truth and Lies. Lies falsely accuses his brother of stealing an imaginary dagger and asks the Ennead to punish Truth by blinding him. After this is done, Lies tells his servants to abandon Truth where he will be torn to pieces by a pride of lions. Instead, they leave him in a thicket of reeds where he is found by the servants of a rich woman. She sleeps with Truth and conceives a son 'who was like the child of a god'.

When this son grows up he tricks Lies into pronouncing his own guilt, just as Seth is tricked in the Contendings. Lies is punished with five open wounds, which seems to mean that his ears and nose were cut off and his eyes were destroyed. Punishments of this kind were actually inflicted on corrupt officials during the New Kingdom.

In another New Kingdom story featuring sibling rivalry, the elder brother is named Anpu (Anubis) and the younger brother is called Bata, the name of a deity sometimes equated with Seth. In 'The Tale of the Two Brothers', Bata cuts off his own penis after being falsely accused of raping his brother's wife. The Ennead creates a mate for Bata but she betrays him and marries a king of Egypt. Bata goes through a series of deaths while in different forms: the flower that contains his heart is destroyed, his bull form is slaughtered and eaten, and his tree form is chopped up and made into furniture. Eventually, Bata is reborn as the son of his former wife, the two brothers are reconciled, and just kingship is re-established.

'Truth and Lies' and 'The Tale of the Two Brothers' should probably not be regarded as disguised or garbled myths, but as stories in which repeating patterns of mythical events were played out by human or semi-human characters. Through ritual and magic, the lives and afterlives of actual Egyptians could also be made to conform with mythical events. How this happened is explored in our last two chapters.

Chapter 9
Personal myths: myth and popular religion

Myths are primarily communal rather than personal narratives. They reflect the values of an entire culture rather than the viewpoint of an individual. Privileged individuals may invent or modify myths but these contributions usually remain anonymous. Myths are often linked to rites benefiting the whole community or its leader, as in the re-enactment of the conflict of Horus and Seth to validate kingship. In Ancient Egypt, myths could also be applied in very personal ways to make a difference in individual lives.

People who were sick or in need of protection were ritually identified with deities in similar situations. Healers and *saw* (protection-makers) added to the stock of myths by combining standard characters and situations, such as 'an infant deity is poisoned' or 'a deity heals in return for a word of power', to suit a particular purpose. Through these spells the sufferings of individuals were transformed into incidents in the war between order and chaos. In some written spells the bare bones of a myth are used; in others they are fleshed out with vivid details and emotional dialogue. Some spells were summarized in visual form. One example is an ivory wand from Thebes made in the 18th century BC and now in the British Museum (Figure 9). Images and text on the wand link a particular person, the 'Lady of the House', Seneb, with solar mythology. Wands of this kind were weapons in a magical defence system for the vulnerable.[1]

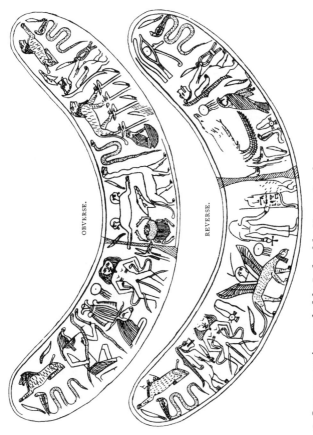

OBVERSE.

REVERSE.

9. Ivory protective wand of the Lady of the House, Seneb

Magical weapons

The objects known as apotropaic wands or magic knives are usually carved out of hippopotamus ivory; a material that was thought to imbue them with power. Seneb's wand is in the shape of a throwstick, a weapon used to kill or stun wild birds, which were classified as creatures of chaos. Apotropaic wands are incised with ferocious-looking figures who may brandish knives or torches. Inscribed examples call these figures gods, fighters, or protectors. According to one inscription, they come to protect by day and by night. Nearly all the inscribed wands were made for women or children. The same kinds of figures decorate a recently excavated birth-brick from Abydos.[2] Egyptian women feared death in childbirth and infant mortality rates were very high. The primary purpose of the wands was to protect pregnant or nursing women and their babies against hostile forces such as demons, ghosts, and sorcerers.

Some wands, judging by their worn or mended condition, were used many times to conjure up protectors for the living. Others were placed in tombs to exercise their protective function in the afterlife and assist the rebirth of the soul. Seneb's wand seems to have been in general use before an inscription was added on top of one of the figures to dedicate the wand to her protection (reverse side, centre).

Many of the images on Seneb's wand, such as the solar disc, the solar eye, the scarab beetle (the god of dawn), the spotted lions of the horizon, and the double sphinx that guards the entrance and exit to the underworld, are linked to the rebirth of the sun after its dangerous journey through the realms of darkness. As we saw in Chapter 8, there was a sequence of myths about the solar child, his divine mother, and the deities who helped to protect them from the forces of evil. The 'Enemies of Ra' are only represented on wands as severed heads, bound captives, or snakes in the process of being stabbed, bitten, or crushed by fighter deities such as the lion-dwarf Aha (later called Bes). The same principle is found on the Metternich Stela, where the infant Horus is shown strangling and trampling the dangerous creatures who threaten him (Figure 2a).

The female figure near the middle of Seneb's wand (reverse side) is clearly a goddess because she holds out an *ankh*. It is likely that a spoken spell was used to identify Seneb temporarily with this goddess. One Middle Kingdom spell for easing childbirth has the doctor or midwife declaim three times, 'It is *Hathor* who is giving birth'. On the birth-brick from Abydos the human mother is shown with the turquoise-blue hair of a goddess. Like a king, Seneb could become part of a repeating pattern of mythical events. Her situation created a temporary link between the divine and human realms. This allowed supernatural powers to fight on behalf of the human mother and baby as if they were fighting for the divine mother and her child. The birth of that child was associated with the daily renewal of the cosmos at sunrise. Through the images on the wand, the fate of the cosmos was bound up with the fate of Seneb.

Images and stories

Although the wand of Seneb is around 1,400 years older than the Metternich Stela, they have many protective beings in common, such as lion deities, the hippopotamus goddess, and the frog goddess (compare Figures 2a-b and 9). The images on the Metternich Stela are complemented by narratives about a specific divine mother and child, Isis and Horus. In these embedded tales, the great goddess Isis experiences the troubles of an ordinary Egyptian woman. She is persecuted by an abusive relative, reduced to poverty, and struggles to obtain justice in a male-dominated system. In one story, Isis turns to the women of the nearest village for help. Versions like this were probably told by village storytellers and would surely have appealed to a female audience.

The texts on ivory wands are brief, but some of the images may stand for specific mythemes. A baboon holding a sacred eye is a common motif on the wands. As we have seen in Chapter 8, this motif can stand for Thoth returning the restored lunar eye to Horus or the pacified solar eye to Ra. The feline creatures shown on many wands could represent the Great Cat who traditionally slew the chaos monster Apophis under a tree at Heliopolis, or the wandering eye goddess in her unpacified form. Brutal images on some wands of cats or lions devouring foreigners may allude to the myth of the eye goddess being sent by Ra to destroy the evil portion of humanity.

It seems likely that stories about such 'fighter' deities were told as part of the protective ritual in which the wands were used. The women and children in need of protection were more likely to feel reassured if they knew something about the beings who were invoked to guard them. For much of Egyptian history, such 'old wives' tales' would have been considered too low in status to be recorded in writing. This may be why the dwarf god Bes and the hippopotamus goddess Taweret, who are commonly shown on objects used in daily life, scarcely feature in Egyptian literature. It is difficult to assess how much ordinary Egyptians knew about myth because of the dominance exercised by the state over religious art and language.

Popular religion

There were strict rules about what could be shown on religious buildings and objects, even those belonging to private people. These rules did gradually become less restrictive. During the 3rd millennium BC, deities were shown with kings but hardly ever with lesser people. Old Kingdom tombs were decorated with many scenes of daily life, but people were not shown in temples worshipping gods. However, Old Kingdom personal names often incorporated divine names (as in Nefer-seshem-Ra – 'Beautiful is the conduct of Ra'), and tomb inscriptions reveal that many elite men and women served in temples as part-time priests and priestesses.

During the Middle Kingdom, the provincial governors who were also part-time high priests showed religious festivals on their tomb walls, but the deities involved were only represented by sacred objects. The Coffin Texts used in some elite burials of this era (see, for example, Figure 5) do form one of the major sources for Egyptian myth. In the late Middle Kingdom and the Second Intermediate Period, deities began to appear on expensive private objects, such as coffins, votive stelae, and the ivory wands. The wand of Seneb is particularly interesting because it resembles a royal Underworld Book reduced to two sets of images.

During the New Kingdom, it became generally acceptable for living people to be shown making offerings to divine statues or sacred animals, and for dead people to be shown in the presence of the gods of the underworld. In Egyptian polytheism everyone, whatever their age, gender, status, or occupation, could find a face of the divine that seemed relevant to them. Egyptian intellectuals searched for ways of expressing the relationship between the one creator god and the many other deities, but in most periods the worship of one deity does not seem to have been considered morally superior. The ideal pious Egyptian followed the ethical code of *maat* and honoured as many deities as possible by making offerings, taking part in festivals, serving as a part-time priest or priestess, and contributing to the repair or building of shrines.

Myth at Deir el-Medina

Much of our knowledge of popular religion comes from New Kingdom Deir el-Medina, the village of the royal tomb-builders. There was an unusually high literacy rate in this community. Its wealthier members are known to have owned mythical narratives, such as the 'Contendings of Horus and Seth' (Figure 7). Some drawings by the villagers seem to illustrate fables, with animals as the main characters. These drawings are hundreds of years older than the earliest known written versions of such fables.

Through working on the royal tombs, the men of Deir el-Medina would have become familiar with the contents of 'secret' Underworld Books describing the mystic journey of the sun god. This knowledge was put to practical use. The epic mythical image of the Night Boat of Ra surviving the attacks of the Apophis serpent was invoked in written spells to deal with the snake and scorpion bites that were a hazard of working life. The most elaborate anti–venom spell found at Deir el-Medina includes 'The Secret Name of Ra', the story in which Isis poisons the sun god and tricks him into passing on the power that went with knowledge of his true name.

Myth-based calendars were used at Deir el-Medina. These seem to be adapted from temple calendars, but they had a similar function to horoscopes. They classify days or parts of days as lucky or unlucky according to which mythical events were believed to have taken place on them. According to the 'Cairo Calendar', the 22nd day of the first month of Akhet (the inundation season) was the mainly unlucky day on which Horus fought Seth, Isis harpooned Seth, and Horus became angry with his mother. These are the incidents described in detail in the Contendings. The 26th day of the third month of Akhet was the lucky day on which Horus and Seth were reconciled and the Black Land was given to Horus and the Red Land to Seth.

Some calendars include predictions of a surprisingly specific nature. An entry in Papyrus Sallier IV for the day on which the Ennead was created (through the sexual power of Atum) warns that a man born on this day will die while having sex. If the occupants of Deir el-Medina had taken these calendars too literally, the royal tombs would never have been finished. They may have been used as a guide to when to take magical precautions, such as wearing a protective amulet.

One warning was against travelling on the day of the feast which 'Ra made to pacify Sekhmet'. This is an allusion to the story of Ra changing his mind after sending his eye in the form of the lion-goddess Sekhmet to destroy humanity. Another probable reference to this myth occurs on a stela dedicated by a draftsman called Neferabu who worked at Deir el-Medina in the 13th century BC.[3] This is one of a type known as penitential stelae because they are inscribed with prayers that ask a deity for forgiveness. In his inscription, Neferabu admits that he was too ignorant and stupid to know right from wrong. He committed an (unspecified) crime against a local cobra-goddess called Meretseger. She punished him with an affliction that he says was as painful as childbirth. Neferabu warns others that Meretseger will attack the guilty man like a savage lion, but she can be appeased by prayers and offerings. As an individual, Neferabu places himself among the guilty portion of humanity who deserved to be punished but, as in the myth, the creator was merciful and the avenging lion-goddess was transformed into a gracious goddess as welcome as 'a sweet breeze on a hot day'.

Amulets and bronzes

The Greeks and Romans frequently used mythological scenes to decorate secular objects. Most Egyptian art had a religious or magical purpose and mythological motifs were sparingly applied. In the Third Intermediate Period, there was a major increase in the number and type of non-royal objects incorporating such motifs. It is probably no coincidence that this change took place at a time when the priesthood was particularly powerful and Egypt was no longer united under strong kings.

Mythological scenes, such as the separation of the earth from the sky, started to appear in private funerary papyri and on coffins.

Amulets in the form of deities became much more common, and the most elaborate sacred eye amulets date from this era (see Figure 8). Some amulet types, such as Horus harpooning, or Isis and baby Horus in a papyrus thicket, depict scenes from myths. A pendant made for a Libyan chieftain who had settled in the Delta shows the sun god in his day boat attended by his daughters, Hathor and Maat. An inscription names the solar deity as 'Amun-Ra-Horakhty who sails the heavens to protect Sheshonq'.[4] The great solar cycle is treated as taking place to save one individual, rather as Christians have been encouraged to believe that Jesus Christ died for them personally.

During the Late and Graeco-Roman Periods, it became customary for wealthier individuals to dedicate bronze statuettes of deities in temples. Some of these votive bronzes comprise mythical tableaux such as the infant sun god emerging from the primeval lotus, or the creator bringing together the Ogdoad. The donors who paid for these bronzes were unlikely to choose a figure or scene that they knew nothing about. Attending temple festivals that included re-enactments or recitations of myths was one way that familiarity with myths could have been acquired.

Temples and festivals

The Metternich Stela and the Shabaqo Stone provide two examples of mythological texts displayed in temples. The narratives embedded in spells on the Metternich Stela may have been read aloud for sufferers from snake and scorpion bites who sought healing in the temple. The creation account in the Memphite Theology may have been read out during foundation ceremonies and at the New Year festival when the cosmos needed to be renewed. It is not clear how public such recitations were. There was no congregation to witness the daily ritual of offering and praise carried out in any Egyptian temple, as the inner areas of a temple could only be entered by people in a state of ritual purity. Access to the cult statue, in which the deity was thought to reside, was restricted to the king and high-ranking priests and priestesses.

During major festivals, the cult image might be placed in a miniature boat and taken into areas of the temple complex that were accessible to the public or even on a visit to another temple. The festival of Sokar, a god of regeneration, involved dragging a boat shrine through the cemeteries of Memphis. During the festival of Min, a deity linked with agricultural fertility, the god's statue visited grain fields and lettuce gardens. These festivals gave the local population a rare opportunity to get close to a physical manifestation of a deity. Food and drink often seem to have been distributed to the crowd as part of the celebrations.

Scenes and inscriptions on the walls of the temple of Horus at Edfu have been interpreted as a 'mystery play' on the theme of the conflict between Horus and Seth. Some of the episodes, such as Horus harpooning Seth, seem to have been acted out on the temple lake. The crowd could have been given a role to play. At many temples there was a festival to celebrate the return of the wandering eye goddess to Egypt. Graffiti and rock inscriptions record that people went out into the desert to help bring home the goddess, as Thoth and Shu did in the myth. In the story of the 'Destruction of Humanity', Ra distracts the eye goddess from slaughtering the remainder of humanity by making her drunk on beer dyed to look like blood. Emulating the goddess by getting very drunk seems to have been a major feature of festivals celebrating Hathor, 'Lady of Intoxication'. The warning not to travel on the day of the feast that Ra made to transform Sekhmet into Hathor was probably a very sensible one.

At Bubastis in the Delta, the ferocious eye/lion goddess was transformed during a festival into a benign cat goddess of fertility. The Greek historian Herodotus (c.484–420 BC) has left us a vivid account of the drunkness, music-making, and bawdy good humour that were a part of this festival. He mentions that women sailing to

Box 12

SOME TEMPLE FESTIVALS LINKED TO MYTHS

Festival	Temple	Myth
Intoxication	Mut temple, Karnak; Bubastis	Destruction of humanity
Khoiak	Abydos etc.	Death and resurrection of Osiris
Opet	Luxor	Union of hand goddess and creator/royal birth myth
Potter's wheel	Esna	Creation of life by Khnum
Return	Medamud etc.	Return of the Distant Goddess
Victory	Edfu	Triumph of Horus over Seth

Some major festivals, such as the Beautiful Festival of the Wadi in Thebes, do not seem to have any associated myths. During this festival, the boat shrine of Amun-Ra visited the west bank to unite with Hathor, Lady of the Necropolis, and bring new life to the dead. A story in Papyrus Vandier in which a brave courtier voluntarily enters the realm of Hathor, queen of the underworld, in place of his king might be based on myth relating to this festival that has not survived in narrative form.

the festival would pull up their dresses to display their genitals to people on the bank – the same gesture that Hathor used in the Contendings to arouse the creator sun god from his torpor. These ordinary Egyptian women were merrily playing the most important of all goddess roles in myth: that of the partner who stimulated the creation and renewal of life.

Herodotus also claimed that Egyptian peasant women paraded a phallic puppet of Osiris around the local fields to make the crops grow. The most profound of all Egyptian festivals were those which re-enacted the death, burial, and resurrection of Osiris. The mythology of death, and its central place in Egyptian culture, must form the topic of our last chapter.

Chapter 10

The blessing of the mummy: the mythology of death

The culture and mythology of Ancient Greece has been the inspiration for all kinds of literature. Ancient Egypt has mainly inspired horror stories. Books and films about mummies coming back to life play on a universal fear of the dead. They also provide a safe way of working through such fear. An Egyptian ghost story inscribed on potsherds (*c*.1200 BC) may have been used as part of a spell to exorcize troublesome ghosts. The story tells how a brave high priest spends a night with an angry ghost called Nebusemekh. The high priest promises to transform Nebusemekh's miserable existence by rebuilding his damaged tomb and making regular offerings to his spirit. In this story it is the mummy we are meant to sympathize with. An Ancient Egyptian mummy was a symbol of death and life, fear and hope. This is best illustrated by a type of model mummy known as a corn mummy. The one in Figure 10 is made of river mud, the substance that above all others gave life to Egypt.

The hieroglyph for a recumbent mummy was used at the end of words for sleep and death, implying that both might be temporary states. The hieroglyph showing an upright mummy could be used at the end of words meaning transformation, statue, or likeness. An Egyptian mummy was not just a preserved corpse, it was the transformed image of the person it had once been. Acts such as covering a mummy with sweet-smelling resin or placing a

10. A corn mummy of the Late Period

golden mask over its face helped to turn it into a supernatural being.

At many periods mummies of both genders were identified with Osiris, the archetypal mummy of myth. Model mummies were given the attributes of Osiris, or the falcon head of another god of death and regeneration, Ptah-Sokar-Osiris. Our Late Period corn mummy has a face made of green wax. As ruler of the Underworld, Osiris was usually shown with either green or black skin. These colours came to be interpreted as symbols of agricultural fertility, but may originally have depicted putrefaction.

In the 'Contendings of Horus and Seth', Osiris points out that even stars die and enter his realm. The Contendings is full of sex and violence, but it does not violate the taboo on describing the most terrible of all mythological events: the murder of Osiris by his brother Seth. Attempts by Seth to destroy or steal the body of Osiris could be described in detail; the assault that led to Osiris becoming a corpse could not. In the Pyramid Texts of the Old Kingdom, Osiris, ruler of Egypt, is merely said to have been 'laid on his side'. He or his son bring a case before a divine tribunal. The tribunal rules that Osiris is justified in his complaint against Seth. Osiris is 'raised up', but his fate is to become the ruler of the underworld. It is his son, Horus who will be ruler of the living. Justice has been done, but the horror of untimely death is not denied. In a dialogue in the Book of the Dead (Spell 175), Osiris laments that he is forced to dwell in a grim place, divided from those he loves. The creator responds that Osiris has been compensated with the gift of power over all beings.

The Memphite Theology does state that Osiris was drowned, but quickly goes on to recount how Isis recovered his body from beneath the water. A New Kingdom hymn to Osiris as King of the Gods glosses over his death with a vague reference to the 'acts of the disturber' (Seth). It concentrates on how Isis found the lost body of Osiris and temporarily restored it to life so that she could conceive

Horus. In this strand of thought, the resurrection of Osiris is an erection that enables his seed to begin the creative process. This kind of sexual symbolism for the renewal of life was widespread. In some Underworld Books the light of the sun gives the mummies of the virtuous dead erections. Corn mummies are usually ithyphallic, and the penises of the elite dead, such as Tutankhamun, were mummified in an upright position.

In his book about Isis and Osiris, the Greek writer Plutarch (c.AD 46–126) reported a tradition that held that the penis was the one part of the dismembered body of Osiris which Isis had failed to find, so she had had to make him a false one. Plutarch gives the longest extant account of the murder of Osiris. He relates how jealous Typhon (Seth) tricked his brother Osiris into climbing into an open coffin. The coffin was sealed with molten metal and thrown into the Nile. It was swept out into the Mediterranean and eventually washed ashore in Byblos in the Lebanon. A miraculous tree grew up concealing the coffin. The king of Byblos had the tree cut down to make into a pillar for his palace. The grieving Isis traced the coffin to Byblos. She found work in the palace as a hairdresser and children's nurse so that she could be near her murdered husband. Eventually, Isis revealed her divinity to the king and queen, who gave her the coffin to take back to Egypt. There it was discovered by Seth, who tore the body of Osiris to pieces.

This account has no exact parallel in Egyptian, but Plutarch may have been drawing on local traditions and popular tales. At Herakleopolis, for example, the *ba* of the dead Osiris was supposed to emerge from a sacred tree. As early as the Middle Kingdom, Sobek was said to have crossed the Great Green (the Mediterranean) to search for the body of Osiris. The way in which Isis is reduced to working as a servant is similar to her plight in stories about the infancy of Horus inscribed on the Metternich Stela. In all these narratives, Isis is portrayed as experiencing anguish, loneliness, and fear for the future like any human widow. These emotions were also given voice in poetic laments that were recited or sung by women playing the roles of Isis and her sister Nephthys at funerals and Osiris festivals.

Funerals and festivals

In the Pyramid Texts, dead kings were 'raised up' like Osiris. This identification with the fate of Osiris spread through the elite class until any dead person could be referred to as 'the Osiris so and so'. By the New Kingdom many elements of embalming and funeral rituals were associated, via words, gestures, or images, with the myth of Osiris. Anubis was said to have turned the body of Osiris into the first mummy, which was protected by the magic charms of Thoth. Scenes on funerary stelae, coffins, or tomb walls show the deceased attended by a figure with the jackal-head of Anubis. Sometimes this appears to be a priest wearing a jackal-mask, sometimes the figure is named as the god himself. The 'Books of Breathing', placed in burials from the 4th century BC onwards, were said to have been written by Isis and Thoth for use by Osiris.

In funeral processions the son of the deceased or a funerary priest played the role of Horus giving his father a new lease of life in the underworld. Offerings made to the dead were equated with the life-giving eye of Horus that revived Osiris. The two weeping women who kept a vigil over the mummy and accompanied the cortège were identified as the 'Two Kites': Isis and Nephthys mourning their lost brother/husband. These identifications have led to spirited arguments over whether such rites were designed to fit existing myths, or whether elements of the myths arose to explain archaic funerary rituals. Probably sometimes the myth came first and sometimes the ritual, but this answer is not acceptable to proponents of the opposing schools who are as difficult to reconcile as Horus and Seth.

Some Egyptians set up cenotaphs or funerary stelae, or buried small mummiform figurines of themselves in the great cemetery and pilgrimage centre of Abydos. This enabled their spirits to take part in the annual festival of Osiris, in which the god's death and resurrection were partially re-enacted. Inscriptions left at Abydos by Middle Kingdom royal officials make it clear that crowds took part in a symbolic combat. A boat shrine containing an image of the god travelled from his palace (temple) to his 'tomb' and back again. Along the way, the god was attacked by enemies who had to be vigorously repulsed. Accounts of similar festivals of the 1st millennium BC claim that people were injured or even killed in such combats.

By this period, most major temples had a 'tomb' of Osiris in their precincts where the local populace could dedicate corn mummies or figurines of the god by burying them in miniature tomb-chambers. Temple texts describe goddesses making mummiform figures to magically assist Osiris to rise again. Actual corn mummies, like the one in Figure 10, were made out of mud or sand mixed with seeds of barley or emmer-wheat. These mummies were sometimes buried in ravines on the edge of the desert. When they were watered by a flash flood or a rain storm, the seeds would grow and life would come out of death.[1]

From at least as early as the Middle Kingdom, the death and regeneration of Osiris had been specifically linked to the annual cycle of the sowing and harvesting of food crops. Barley was said to spring from the ribs of his body, and the donkeys who threshed corn with their hooves and carried grain on their backs were reviled as creatures of Seth. The use of the *wedjat* eye measure for grain ties in with the idea that crops came from the body of Osiris after it was regenerated through the presentation of the eye of Horus. Since bread made from corn and beer made from barley were the basic foodstuffs for all Egyptians, the regeneration of Osiris was important to the whole nation.

From the New Kingdom onwards, Osiris beds (wooden outlines of the god filled with soil) and corn mummies were also placed in tombs. They were sometimes watered during the funeral so that the seeds would sprout after the tomb was closed. Such symbolism helped to incorporate the human dead in a great cycle of death and regeneration that encompassed all created beings and things. The human dead were also expected to play an active role in the maintenance of the cycle initiated by the creator.

An awfully big adventure

Peter Pan's description of death as 'an awfully big adventure' would have made sense to any Ancient Egyptian. People like the physician Gua expected to face many dangers in the transitional period after death. As one of the wealthy elite, he could afford decorated and inscribed burial equipment that would help him to deal with these dangers. Like deities, the dead were thought to have a variety of manifestations, so that they could be present in several places and bodies at once. While Gua's mummy lay protected in its set of coffins, his bird-like *ba* would travel through the *duat*. Gua had maps so that he could follow the route taken by the sun god on his nightly voyage (Figure 5) and spells to get him past guardian demons and to persuade divine ferrymen to take him where he needed to go.

The spell collection known as the Coffin Texts resembles a 'Worst Case Scenario Handbook' for the afterlife. The dead were afraid of suffering thirst and hunger, of being lost in darkness, attacked by snakes, burned by divine fire, caught and dismembered by demons, or forced to walk upside-down eating excrement and drinking urine. Most of these vividly imagined horrors could be avoided through mythological role-playing. A deceased person such as Gua could claim to be returning the lost eye of Horus like Thoth, supporting the sky like Shu, or repelling the Apophis monster from the sun boat like Seth. A great variety of such transitory identifications were used to give the deceased the power or knowledge they were thought to need in a particular situation. As deities succeeded in their divine travels, so would the deceased.

By the New Kingdom, the more compact spell collection now known as the Book of the Dead had replaced the Coffin Texts. In the Book of the Dead, prominence was given to the ordeal of judgement before the divine tribunal. The 42 judges sat in the throneroom of Osiris, the Hall of the Double Maat. The deceased had to suffer the scrutiny of this divine tribunal, as Osiris and Horus had once done. After the deceased had made a declaration of innocence, his or her heart was weighed against an image of Maat, the goddess of Truth. Like Ra, the virtuous were thought to carry Maat in their hearts. Bearing in mind the difficulty that even gods had in obtaining justice, the dead were allowed to use magic. A scarab carved with a spell that stopped the heart from reporting any evil it contained might be placed on or in a mummy's chest. The desired verdict was to be found 'true of voice' as Osiris had been. Like Osiris, the virtuous dead could not return to their old life on earth. They had to take on new forms and dwell in new realms.

Ultimate destinations

In the Coffin Texts, the deceased might be imagined as living in the Field of Reeds where corn grew to giant size, receiving all good things in the Field of Offerings, dwelling with Thoth in the Mansion of the Moon, or joining the retinue of the great goddess Hathor. Coffin Text 1130 describes an entire cycle from the creation of the world by the 'Lord of All' to its ending when the creator will become at one with the 'Inert One' (Osiris). It finishes by promising that anyone who knows this spell will exist like Osiris in the underworld and Ra in the east, unharmed by divine fire. Resting with Osiris and travelling with Ra were the two main fates of the 'justified' dead.

An early belief linking the spirits of the dead with the circumpolar stars implies a fear of entering the realm of Osiris. These stars were the only ones that did not periodically set below the horizon and 'rest with Osiris'. In the 'Contendings of Horus and Seth', the court of Osiris is peopled with terrifying messengers of death. Osiris claims that Maat has been forced to come and live with him because

Egypt has become corrupt. From the Old Kingdom to the Roman Period, it is possible to find Egyptian texts which stress that a happy afterlife was dependent on ethical behaviour rather than on being able to afford the best tomb and funerary equipment.

This point was graphically made in a story that was probably composed in the late 1st millennium BC. It tells how a prince called Setna watches two funeral processions, one of a rich man who is going to be buried with the best of everything and one of a poor man who will be dumped in the desert with no burial goods at all. Setna's son uses magic to take his father into the underworld to find out the fate of the two men. Both are judged in the court of Osiris. The rich man is found to have been wicked and selfish, and is condemned to eternal torture. The poor man is judged to have lived a good life. He is given all the rich man's burial goods, which help him to become a blessed spirit in the following of Osiris.

As this ethical view of the afterlife gained in popularity, Osiris and Isis became less ambiguous figures in myth. Osiris developed into the good ruler, the embodiment of injured innocence and ultimate justice. Isis became the perfect wife and mother, taking on the task of saving all humanity as she had once saved her husband and son from extinction.

All in the same boat

The emphasis on family loyalties in the myths of Osiris, Isis, and Horus is a pointer to the way that ordinary Egyptians thought about their dead. Everyone who died was a potential *akh*, a transfigured spirit with semi-divine powers. Letters written to dead people make it clear that individuals were thought to retain their personalities and family ties beyond the grave. The passage in the Contendings in which the dead Osiris helps his son to gain the throne reflects the way that Egyptians expected their dead relatives to use their power and influence to assist family members.

Box 13

UNDERWORLD BOOKS

The Pyramid Texts (24th century BC onwards), the Coffin Texts (*c.*22nd century BC onwards), and the Book of the Dead (16th century BC onwards) are diverse collections of funerary spells. No two copies were the same. The illustrated Underworld Books were complete compositions centred on the voyages of the sun god. The major Underworld Books copied onto the walls and ceilings of royal tombs and cenotaphs include:

Amduat ('What is in the Underworld'), 15th century BC or earlier
The sun god and his crew journey through the twelve hours of darkness.

Litany of Ra, 15th century BC
An invocation of the 75 forms of the sun god in the underworld.

Book of Gates, 14th century BC or earlier
The sun god, Sia (creative thought), and Heka (magic) journey through the twelve gates of the underworld.

Books of Night and Day, 14th century BC
The sun god and his crew travel through the body of the sky goddess, Nut.

Book of Caverns, 13th century BC
The sun god journeys through the twelve caverns of the underworld to unite with Osiris.

Book of the Earth, 13th century BC
The transformations of the sun god in the underworld.

Many of these books were later adapted for use on non-royal tomb walls, coffins, and funerary papyri. Some of the underworld imagery may have influenced early Christian ideas about hell.

Pharaonic culture, on the other hand, was dependent on Egyptians putting king and country before family loyalties. In the funerary texts associated with the solar cult, the dead are treated as part of the larger society of Egypt and the divine order. Dead people were divided into 'Enemies of Ra' and 'Excellent spirits of Ra'. The Enemies of Ra feature in the Underworld Books on the walls of royal tombs being beheaded, burned, or boiled alive.

In these Underworld Books even the most powerful kings appear in merely supporting roles (see Box 13). Their fate after death is subsumed in the fate of the night sun as he travels the river of the underworld in his boat. The renewal of the cosmos depended on the crew of the sun boat. One name for this vessel was the 'Boat of Millions'. From the Middle Kingdom onwards, the non-royal dead could aspire to join this crew and take part in the vital work of sailing and defending the boat from dusk to dawn. There were funerary spells for 'Getting aboard the Boat of Ra' and for 'Becoming the swiftest rower in the Boat of Ra'. Illustrated spells show deceased people taking on the roles of mighty deities such as Seth or the eye goddess in order to slay the chaos monsters who threatened the sun boat. The afterlife became an eternal voyage, with humanity literally all in the same boat.

The light shed by the sun god as he passed through the underworld was said to waken the mummies of the justified dead from their sleep-like state. Poignantly, the light only lasted for a single hour, but for the dead this apparently seemed like a whole lifetime spent in the Field of Reeds. Several realities are posited, operating on different timescales.

Some Underworld Books revealed the 'secret knowledge' that Ra and Osiris, life and death, were really one. The two gods merged in the mid-point of the night and the cycle of death and regeneration began again. Dawn, the beautiful moment celebrated by objects as diverse as the majestic obelisk known as Cleopatra's Needle and the wand of the housewife, Seneb, would bring the renewal of life.

Notes

Chapter 1

1. For more on obelisks, see Labib Habachi, *The Obelisks of Egypt: Skyscrapers of the Past* (Cairo, 1984) and A. Noakes, *Cleopatra's Needles* (London, 1962).
2. All the quotations are from A. H. Gardiner, 'Hymns to Sobek in a Ramesseum Papyrus', *Revue d'Egyptologie* 11, 1957: 43–56. Despite his scornful attitude, Gardiner was a pioneering translator who made many important contributions to the study of Egyptian myth.

Chapter 2

1. For the history of the Metternich Stela, see N. E. Scott in *Bulletin of the Metropolitan Museum of Art*, April 1951, pp. 201–17, and for its texts see C. E. Sander-Hansen, *Die Texte der Metternich Stele* (Copenhagen, 1956) and J. F. Borghouts, *Ancient Egyptian Magical Texts* (Leiden, 1978).

Chapter 3

1. This statue (no. 107), and other finds from the temple of Sobek of Sumenu, are described in J. Romano, *The Luxor Museum of Ancient Egyptian Art* (Cairo, 1979).

Chapter 4

1. A full English translation of the inscriptions can be found in M. Lichtheim, *Ancient Egyptian Literature*, vol. I, pp. 51–7.

2. K. Sethe, in *Das 'Denkmal memphitischer Theologie' der Schabakostein des Britischen Museums* (Leipzig, 1928) and H. Junker, in *Die Götterlehre von Memphis* (Berlin, 1940).

Chapter 5

1. For more information on the coffins of Gua, go to *www.thebritishmuseum.ac.uk/compass*.
2. The only full translation is J. Vandier, *Le Papyrus Jumilhac* (Paris, 1961), but some sections are translated in an appendix to S. Tower Hollis, *The Ancient Egyptian 'Tale of Two Brothers': The Oldest Fairy Tale in the World* (Norman and London, 1990).

Chapter 6

1. In Joseph Campbell, *The Masks of God: Oriental Mythology* (New York, 1962), pp. 49–102.

Chapter 7

1. For a selection of these interpretations, see the works listed in Further reading and also S. A. Allam, 'Legal Aspects in the "Contendings of Horus and Seth"', in *Studies in Pharaonic Religion and Society in Honour of J. Gwyn Griffiths*, ed. A. B. Lloyd (London, 1992), pp. 137–45; M. Broze, *Mythe et roman en Égypte ancienne; Les aventures d'Horus et Seth dans le papyrus Chester Beatty I* (Leuven, 1996); F. Junge, 'Mythos und Literarizität. Die Geschichte vom Streit der Götter Horus und Seth', in *Quaerentes Scientiam: Festgabe für Wolfhart Westendorf*, ed. H. Behlmer (Göttingen, 1994), pp. 83–101; J. Spiegel, *Die Erzählung vom Streite des Horus und Seth in Pap. Beatty I als Literaturwerk* (Glückstadt, 1937); D. Sweeney, 'Gender and Conversational Tactics in *The Contendings of Horus and Seth*', *Journal of Egyptian Archaeology*, 88 (2002): 141–62.
2. In W. K. Simpson (ed.), *The Literature of Ancient Egypt* (New Haven and London, 1972), p. 108.
3. Rock drawings and inscriptions are published in J. C. Darnell, *Theban Desert Road Survey in the Egyptian Desert* (Chicago, 2002).

4. U. Verhoeven, 'Eine historischer "Sitz in Leben" für den Erzählung von Horus und Seth des Papyrus Chester Beatty I', in *Wege öffnen. Festschrift für Rolf Grundlach*, ed. M. Schade-Busch (Wiesbaden, 1996), pp. 361–3.

Chapter 9

1. For more on the wands and how they were used, see F. Legge, 'The Magic Ivories of the Middle Empire', *Proceedings of the Society for Biblical Archaeology*, May 1905: 130–52; and G. Pinch, *Magic in Ancient Egypt* (London, 1994).
2. The bricks were used to raise and support women during childbirth. See J. Wegner, 'A decorated birth-brick from South Abydos', *Egyptian Archaeology*, 21, autumn 2002: 3–4.
3. The stela of Neferabu and several other texts from Deir el-Medina mentioned in this book are translated by A. G. McDowell in *Village Life in Ancient Egypt: Laundry Lists and Love Songs* (New York, 1999).
4. This jewel was buried with King Sheshonq II at Tanis. See F. Tiradritti (ed.), *The Cairo Museum Masterpieces of Egyptian Art* (London, 1998), pp. 330, 332–3.

Chapter 10

1. For more on corn mummies and related objects, see M. Raven, 'Corn mummies', *Oudheidkundige Mededelingen uit het Rijksmuseum te Leiden*, 63, 1982: 7–38; and A. M. J. Tooley, 'Osiris Bricks', *Journal of Egyptian Archaeology*, 82, 1996: 167–79.

Further reading

Translations of Egyptian myths

English translations of most of the myths mentioned in this book can be found in the following anthologies: M. Lichtheim, *Ancient Egyptian Literature*, vols. I–III (Berkeley, 1973–80); R. B. Parkinson, *The Tale of Sinuhe and Other Ancient Egyptian Poems 1940–1640* BC (Oxford, 1997); J. B. Pritchard (ed.), *Ancient Near Eastern Texts Relating to the Old Testament* (Princeton, 1950, 1955); and W. K. Simpson (ed.), *The Literature of Ancient Egypt* (New Haven and London, 1972).

Translations of funerary sources for myth include: T. G. Allen, *The Book of the Dead or the Book of Going Forth by Day* (Chicago, 1974); R. O. Faulkner, *The Ancient Egyptian Pyramid Texts* (Warminster, n.d.), and *The Ancient Egyptian Coffin Texts*, vols. I–III (Warminster, 1973–8); and for Underworld Books, A. Piankoff, *The Tomb of Ramesses VI*, vols. I–II (New York, 1954). There is a detailed list of translations of major mythological texts in G. Pinch, *Handbook of Egyptian Mythology* (Santa Barbara, 2002), pp. 233–8.

General references

For general discussions of Egyptian myth, see J. Baines, 'Egyptian Myth and Discourse: Myth, Gods, and the Early Written and Iconographic Record', *Journal of Near Eastern Studies*, 50, 1991: 81–105; J. van Dijk, 'Myth and Mythmaking in Ancient Egypt', in J. M. Sasson (ed.),

Civilizations of the Ancient Near East, vol. III (New York, 1995),
   pp.1697–1709; K. Goebs, 'A Functional Approach to Egyptian Myth and
   Mythemes', *Journal of Ancient Near Eastern Religions*, 2, 2002: 27–59;
   and G. Hart, *Egyptian Myths* (London, 1990).

Chapter 1

E. Hornung, *The Secret Lore of Egypt: Its Impact on the West*,
   tr. D. Lorton (Ithaca and London, 2001).

E. Iversen, *The Myth of Egypt and its Hieroglyphs in European
   Tradition* (Princeton, 1993).

R. Parkinson, *Cracking Codes: The Rosetta Stone and Decipherment*
   (London 1999).

Chapter 2

J. P. Allen, *Middle Egyptian: An Introduction to the Language and
   Culture of Hieroglyphs* (Cambridge, 2000).

A. Loprieno (ed.), *Ancient Egyptian Literature: History and Forms*
   (Leiden and New York, 1996).

P. Wilson, *Sacred Signs: Hieroglyphs in Ancient Egypt* (Oxford,
   2003).

Chapter 3

J. Assmann, *The Search for God in Ancient Egypt*, tr. D. Lorton (Ithaca,
   2001).

J. Baines, 'Egyptian Deities in Context: Multiplicity, Unity and the
   Problem of Change', in *One God or Many*, ed. B. Nevling Porter
   (Casco Bay, 2000), pp. 9–78.

E. Hornung, *Conceptions of God in Ancient Egypt: The One and the
   Many*, tr. J. Baines (Ithaca, 1982).

D. Meeks and C. Favard-Meeks, *Daily Life of the Egyptian Gods*, tr.
   G. M. Goshgarian (London and Ithaca, 1996).

R. H. Wilkinson, *The Complete Gods and Goddesses of Ancient Egypt*
   (London, 2003).

Chapter 4

J. P. Allen, *Genesis in Egypt* (San Antonio, 1995).

L. Lesko, 'Ancient Egyptian Cosmogonies and Cosmology', in *Religion in Ancient Egypt: Gods, Myths and Personal Practice*, ed. B. Shafer (Ithaca and London, 1991).

M. Smith, *On the Primeval Ocean* (Copenhagen, 2002).

Chapter 5

J. Baines and J. Malek, *Atlas of Ancient Egypt* (New York, 2000).

R. Friedman (ed.), *Egypt and Nubia: Gifts of the Desert* (London, 2002).

J. F. Richards, 'Conceptual Landscapes in the Egyptian Nile Valley', in *Archaeology of Landscape: Contemporary Perspectives*, eds. W. Ashmore and B. Knapp (Oxford, 1999), pp. 83–100.

P. Vernus, 'The World Order', in his *The Gods of Ancient Egypt* (London and New York, 1998), pp. 65–100.

Chapter 6

L. Bell, *Mythology and Iconography of Divine Kingship in Ancient Egypt* (Chicago, 1994).

H. Frankfort, *Kingship and the Gods* (Chicago, 1948).

D. O'Connor and D. P. Silverman (eds.), *Ancient Egyptian Kingship* (Leiden, 1995).

Chapter 7

A. H. Gardiner, *The Library of A. Chester Beatty: Description of a Hieratic Papyrus with a Mythological Story, Love Songs, and Other Miscellaneous Texts* (London, 1931).

J. W. Griffiths, *The Conflict of Horus and Seth from Egyptian and Classical Sources* (Liverpool, 1960).

R. Oden, 'The Contendings of Horus and Seth (Chester Beatty Papyrus no. 1): A Structural Analysis', *History of Religions*, 18/4, 1979: 352–69.

H. te Velde, 'Relations and Conflicts Between Egyptian Gods: Particularly in the Divine Ennead', in *Struggles of Gods*, ed. H. G. Keppenberg (New York, 1984), pp. 239–57.

Chapter 8

E. Hornung, 'Time and Eternity', tr. E. Bredeck, in *Idea Into Image: Essays on Ancient Egyptian Thought* (Princeton, 1992), pp. 57–71.

H. te Velde, 'Seth and the Eye of Horus', in his *Seth, God of Confusion: A Study of his Role in Egyptian Mythology and Religion* (Leiden, 1977), pp. 46–52.

Chapter 9

J. Baines, 'Practical Religion and Piety', *Journal of Egyptian Archaeology*, 73, 1987: 79–98.

L. H. Lesko (ed.), *Pharaoh's Workers: The Villagers of Deir El Medina* (Ithaca and London, 1994).

S. El-Sabban, *Temple Festival Calendars of Ancient Egypt* (Trowbridge, 2000).

Chapter 10

E. Hornung, *Ancient Egyptian Books of the Afterlife*, tr. D. Lorton (Ithaca, 1999).

S. Ikram and A. Dodson, *The Mummy in Ancient Egypt: Equipping the Dead for Eternity* (London, 1998).

S. Quirke and W. Forman, *Hieroglyphs and the Afterlife* (London, 1996).

J. H. Taylor, *Death and the Afterlife in Ancient Egypt* (London, 2001).

Timeline

(All dates are approximate until the 7th century BC)

Predynastic Period, 5000–3200 BC
Rock drawings
Settlement of Nile Valley
Rise of Upper Egyptian kings

Protodynastic Period, 3200–3100 BC (Dynasty 0)
Creation of hieroglyphic script
Unification of Egypt and founding of Memphis
    (Dynasty 0)

Early Dynastic Period, 3100–2686 BC (Dynasties 1–3)
First connected texts in hieroglyphs

Old Kingdom, 2686–2181 BC (Dynasties 3–6)
Massive royal pyramids built at Giza and Saqqara
    (Dynasties 3–4)
Solar temples built (Dynasty 5)
Pyramid Texts inscribed inside pyramids (Dynasties 5–6)

First Intermediate Period, 2181–2055 BC (Dynasties 7–11)
Egypt split into warring regions
Coffin Texts used in burials of regional elite

Middle Kingdom, 2055–1650 BC (Dynasties 11–13)

Egypt reunited by Nebhepetre Mentuhotep (Dynasty 11)

Egypt becomes a major power in the Near East
  (Dynasty 12)

Golden age of Egyptian literature; first surviving stories and
  Instruction Texts written in hieratic

Key objects: Coffin of Gua and wand of Seneb.

Second Intermediate Period, 1650–1550 BC (Dynasties 13–17)

Egypt divided after foreign incursions

First copies of the Book of the Dead (Dynasty 17)

New Kingdom, 1550–1069 BC (Dynasties 18–20)

Egypt reunited and gains an empire in the Near East
  (Dynasty 18)

Most cult temples rebuilt. Rise of the temple of Amun at Karnak
  (Dynasties 18–20)

Aten briefly replaces all other deities in the Amarna Period.
  Polytheism restored under Tutankhamun (late Dynasty 18)

Long, prosperous reign of Ramesses II (Dynasty 19)

Underworld Books decorate royal tombs in the Valley of the Kings
  (Dynasties 18–20)

Mythical and myth-related narratives written in Late Egyptian
  (Dynasties 19–20)

Key objects: Cleopatra's Needle (obelisk of Thutmose III), statue
  of Amenhotep III and Sobek-Ra, harpooner statuette of
  Tutankhamun, and Papyrus Chester Beatty I.

Third Intermediate Period, 1069–747 BC (Dynasties 21–25)

Egypt frequently divided

Kings of Libyan descent rule from the Delta
  (Dynasties 21–23)

Related dynasty of high priests at Karnak dominate the south
  (Dynasties 21–23)

Invasion by Nubian rulers

Key objects: Sacred eye amulets

Late Period, 747–332 BC (Dynasties 25–30, First and Second Persian Periods)

Egypt reunited under Nubian dynasty (Dynasty 25)

Nubians driven out by Assyrian invasion

Egyptian dynasty from Sais take control (Dynasty 26)

Demotic literature flourishes

Persians conquer Egypt

Egyptian leaders struggle for independence (Dynasties 27–30)

Persians reconquer Egypt

First surviving collections of local myths

Key objects: Shabaqo Stone, corn mummy, and Metternich Stela

Graeco-Roman Period, 332 BC–AD 395 (Macedonian and Ptolemaic Dynasties, Roman Period)

Persian Empire conquered by Alexander the Great. Founding of Alexandria

General Ptolemy takes control of Egypt during the break-up of Alexander's empire

Ptolemy family rules from Alexandria and rebuilds most major Egyptian temples

Myths inscribed on temple walls

Cleopatra VII and her son Caesarion (Ptolemy XV) defeated by Augustus. Egypt becomes part of Roman Empire (30 BC)

Hermetica composed

Egypt gradually becomes Christian

Development of Coptic language and literature

Byzantine (Coptic) Period, AD 395–640

Egypt becomes part of Byzantine Empire

Remaining pagan temples closed down

Knowledge of how to read hieroglyphs lost

Arabs invade Egypt

Arab Period, AD 640–present day

Glossary

Egyptian words are in italics.

akh: a transfigured dead person with semi-divine powers

ankh: the symbol of life

ba: a mobile manifestation of a dead person or deity shown as a human-headed bird

cippus (pl. cippi): a magical stela with an image of a divine child overcoming dangerous creatures

constellation: deities who form a fixed group in a particular context

cosmogony: a history of the origins and development of the universe

Delta: the north of Egypt where the Nile splits up before reaching the sea

duat: the underworld or inner sky; the realm of the dead

ennead: a group of nine deities who may be arranged into generations; a council of deities

hieroglyph: a Greek term meaning sacred carving, used for individual symbols in the pictorial script

Hermetica: texts produced in Graeco-Roman Period Egypt which purported to be the secret teachings of the god Hermes Trismegistus

inundation: the flood caused by the annual rise in water levels of the River Nile

isfet: the evil aspect of chaos

ithyphallic: shown with an erect penis, often of exaggerated size

ka: sustaining spirit of a person or deity

maat: truth, justice, balance, the divine order

nome: an administrative region or province of Egypt

nun: the primeval ocean; a state of watery chaos

ogdoad: a group of primeval deities, usually eight in number

papyrus: a paper made from papyrus stems or a book-scroll made from this paper

pharaoh: a term for an Egyptian king; literal meaning, 'great house' (the palace)

primeval mound: the first land to rise above the primeval waters at creation

scarab: image of a dung-beetle; symbol of Khepri, god of dawn

scribe: a person trained to read and write

shabti (*ushabti*): a magical figurine that acted as a substitute for a deceased person

solar bark: the boat of the sun god, also known as the Boat of Millions

stela: a flat slab with inscriptions and/or images, mainly as set up in tombs or temples

Underworld Books: illustrated texts recording the journeys of the sun god, chiefly found on the walls of royal tombs

uraeus: image of the cobra goddess who protects the king

vignette: an illustration to, or visual summary of, a funerary text

wedjat (*wadjet, udjat*): the restored eye of the god Horus; a symbol of regeneration and wholeness

Index

Page numbers in italic type indicate illustrations

Expand your collection of
VERY SHORT INTRODUCTIONS

Visit the
VERY SHORT
INTRODUCTIONS
Web site

www.oup.co.uk/vsi

➤ **Information** about all published titles

➤ News of **forthcoming books**

➤ **Extracts** from the books, including titles
not yet published

➤ **Reviews** and views

➤ **Links** to other **web sites** and main
OUP web page

➤ Information about **VSIs in translation**

➤ **Contact** the editors

➤ **Order** other **VSIs** on-line

HISTORY
A Very Short Introduction
John H. Arnold

History: A Very Short Introduction is a stimulating essay about how we understand the past. The book explores various questions provoked by our understanding of history, and examines how these questions have been answered in the past. Using examples of how historians work, the book shares the sense of excitement at discovering not only the past, but also ourselves.

'A stimulating and provocative introduction to one of collective humanity's most important quests – understanding the past and its relation to the present. A vivid mix of telling examples and clear cut analysis.'

David Lowenthal, University College London

'This is an extremely engaging book, lively, enthusiastic and highly readable, which presents some of the fundamental problems of historical writing in a lucid and accessible manner. As an invitation to the study of history it should be difficult to resist.'

Peter Burke, Emmanuel College, Cambridge

www.oup.co.uk/vsi/history

ARCHAEOLOGY
A Very Short Introduction
Paul Bahn

This entertaining Very Short Introduction reflects the enduring popularity of archaeology – a subject which appeals as a pastime, career, and academic discipline, encompasses the whole globe, and surveys 2.5 million years. From deserts to jungles, from deep caves to mountain tops, from pebble tools to satellite photographs, from excavation to abstract theory, archaeology interacts with nearly every other discipline in its attempts to reconstruct the past.

'very lively indeed and remarkably perceptive … a quite brilliant and level-headed look at the curious world of archaeology'

Barry Cunliffe, University of Oxford

'It is often said that well-written books are rare in archaeology, but this is a model of good writing for a general audience. The book is full of jokes, but its serious message – that archaeology can be a rich and fascinating subject – it gets across with more panache than any other book I know.'

Simon Denison, editor of *British Archaeology*

www.oup.co.uk/vsi/archaeology